MEDICINAL

CHEF

The
MEDICINAL
CHEF

Eat your way to Managing Diabetes

Tackle Type-1 and Type-2 Diabetes by Changing the Way You Eat, in 50 Recipes

DALE PINNOCK

quadrille

CONTENTS

DIABETES IS ONE OF THE BIG THREE EPIDEMIC-SCALE DISEASES THAT IS PLAGUING THE WESTERN WORLD. IT IS RIFE.

Once a condition that afflicted the unlucky few, diabetes now affects millions. I remember when I was at school, I only knew one person who had it and that was the congenital (born with it) type. Recent figures from Diabetes UK reveal that there are more than *three million* people in the UK now suffering with diabetes. That is 132,000 more than last year! Last *year*. That is a ridiculous increase and almost defies comprehension.

Diabetes UK also state that 90 percent of these cases are type-2 diabetes. That is, from my point of view, what makes it even more alarming, because it is really indicative of environmental issues. We will explore this further in a moment, but in short: type-1 diabetes you are born with, type-2 develops due to a breakdown of normal physiological functions over time and the adaptations that arise because of this. What causes that breakdown? Is it something in the air? No. It is the food that we eat. Whether we like it or not, this disease is on the rise because of what we are doing to ourselves.

Now please don't get me wrong; I'm not standing here in an ivory tower wagging my finger in disdain. I am coming from a point of great concern. There is such a clear need for proper education at a public level that is not tainted or tarnished by industry or watered down by policy makers. I genuinely believe that most of us want to make better choices, but that those choices are being steered by outdated public health messages, or by manufacturers of "food" that is sold under the guise of being a healthy option. Many of the old, well-meaning public health campaigns have caused our diets to change dramatically in composition. What was supposed to have made us healthier has caused the biggest disaster and outright public health mess of all time.

In recent decades, food manufacturers caught onto the flawed public health messages and built brands and multimillion marketing campaigns around them.

So, now that I have painted a little bit of a picture of the horror story that is our current state of health, we should discuss diabetes a little further. As a starting point, let's have a quick look at the distinction between type-1 and type-2.

○ TYPE-1 DIABETES

This is, for the most part, a congenital condition. People are born with it, or it develops in very early childhood (although it does sometimes pop up in adulthood). It is a physical dysfunction of the pancreas that means it is not able to secrete sufficient insulin to keep blood sugar at a safe level. The pancreas is where the hormone insulin is produced. It is the function of insulin to get into the circulation following the consumption of food, to tell the cells of our body that they need to start taking up sugar from the meal to use as energy. There is a two-fold reason for this. Firstly, by telling the cells that there is sugar present, they can take it in and make energy out of it. The second reason is a protective one. Sugar, when it is just in circulation, is potentially very harmful to the body if it is present to excess, so it needs to be shuttled out of the bloodstream when levels get too high. By secreting insulin, we facilitate this. People who have type-1 diabetes have to inject insulin to make up for what their pancreas has become unable to do. Type-1 diabetes arises when the body's own immune system, for reasons yet unknown, attacks a group of specialized cells in the pancreas known as beta cells. They are the cells that manufacture, store, and release insulin when it is needed. As they are damaged by the autoimmune response, they are rendered useless.

⬤ TYPE-2 DIABETES

While still an insulin issue, this is a different animal. This version of the disease means that a person cannot secrete enough insulin or—and certainly more often—that the insulin they do produce doesn't deliver the desired effect. This is really considered to be a lifestyle disease. It is the culmination of a series of events and physiological changes that, aside from a small percentage of hereditary cases, are a result of environmental impacts on body function. By the word environmental, I don't mean exhaust gas, instead I mean the internal environment of the body. The thing that can be massively and profoundly altered by diet and lifestyle.

LIFESTYLE AND DIABETES

To put a perspective on how things have changed in the UK alone, 10 years ago the number of people diagnosed with diabetes was 1.4 million. Now we are at three million. For the rates of a disease to double in such a short space of time, something is very wrong. Is some genetic mutation rearing its head? Increased pollution? Er ... no! It is the major thing that has become rotten in the modern world: our lifestyle, including what we eat.

Poor diet, high levels of stress, and alarming (and increasing) inactivity. That triple whammy cocktail is the catalyst for most of our health woes today. In modern medicine we have, in many ways, become miracle workers. The myriad infectious illnesses that used to plague us and wipe us out in our 30s are history. If you get hit by a bus, you can get patched up by the best surgical procedures imaginable. If your appendix gets infected, then it gets taken out without so much as a blink. There are drug treatments that can cure, prevent, or manage almost everything. With all this, we should be in profound good health. But we are in the midst of a crisis.

That's because there is one thing modern medicine cannot do: it cannot stop us killing ourselves. This may sound preachy or hyperbolic, but it is most certainly true. When it comes to the modern diseases afflicting us at an alarming rate—aside from a very small percentage where heredity is involved—we are in the driving seat. We can take small steps that can have a profound impact upon our health in both the short and the long term. Modern medicine has a very poor track record in terms of managing these conditions; the best that can be done is to attempt to manage some of the symptoms or outcomes. But, so far, it does so very poorly.

The biggest public health crises in the modern world really need all of us to do all we can to keep them at bay. We need to understand how our lifestyle influences our health, how it can put us at risk of these big killers, and, most importantly of all, what we can start doing *today* to improve the picture for ourselves.

ABOUT THIS BOOK

This book aims to give you the key information surrounding what you can do to help manage your diabetes. This isn't about cures or making false promises. I simply intend to show you what we understand today in regard to the science of nutrition and its relationship to diabetes. I also aim to put that information across in a concise, digestible, and—most important of all—practical and enjoyable format, so you can learn about the condition painlessly. Rather than swamp you with science and leave you blindly stumbling in the wilderness to figure out how to apply it, I have put the information you will learn into the most practical and applicable format of all: food!

One thing I have to admit from the get-go is this: there is a massive slant toward type-2 diabetes in this book. This is for the simple reason that, in terms of the pathology, there is more that we have the potential to control in type-2 diabetes. Type-2 diabetes is a slow, gradual series of changes that result in a dangerous outcome. If we remove some of the factors that are adding to the problem, we can make great positive strides.

For type-1 diabetes, the information here absolutely does stand up 100 percent, but always bear in mind that it is a permanent condition and no diet in the world will correct it. Though obviously, if you are a type-1 diabetes sufferer, you must be very conscious of your diet every day to manage your condition successfully and this book will indeed give you those tools.

KEY ANATOMY AND PHYSIOLOGY

To really understand the impact that your diet has upon your health and how it may relate to your specific health concerns, you need to be as informed as possible and to learn as much as you can about how it all works.

That is why we need to look at the background science a little bit here, paying particular attention to the structure and function of different tissues.

Structures and functions will be very important things to understand later on when it comes to actually putting all the pieces together and having this information down-pat for life. I want to give you enough information to empower you and help you to understand your body and your health a little better, but at the same time not to overload you.

So let's begin with the base structure of every tissue in your body. That is your …

CELLS

Cells are the smallest living components of our body, yet are some of the most mind-blowing and complex pieces of wizardry imaginable. They are the small components inside us that collectively make up the many tissues in the various different systems of our body. There are thousands of different types of cells in the body with all manner of weird and wonderful adaptations and specialized variations, and our bodies are composed of an estimated 37.2 trillion of them.

As a completely living unit, cells can replicate, regulate almost every aspect of their function, and even suss out when is the best time to die for the good of the rest of the body. That's pretty impressive! There are several components that make up the structure of each of our cells and familiarity with these will be very useful later on.

THE MEMBRANE

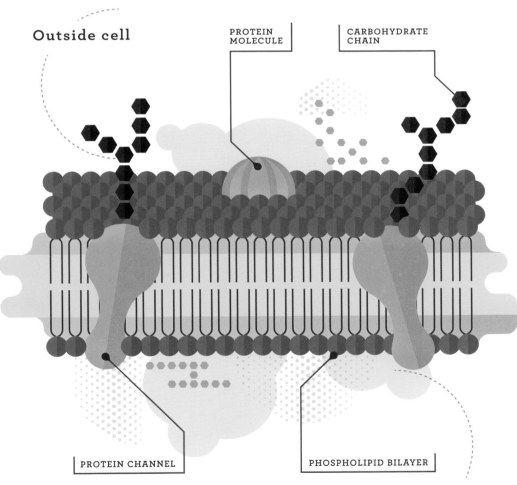

Outside cell

PROTEIN MOLECULE

CARBOHYDRATE CHAIN

PROTEIN CHANNEL

PHOSPHOLIPID BILAYER

Inside cell

THE MEMBRANE

The membrane is the flexible active outer bubble that separates all the intricate workings of the inside of the cell from the outer environment. The cell membrane is made from what is known as a phospholipid bilayer. This is a layer of two lipid (fatty) molecules back-to-back in a continuous sheet that surrounds the whole cell, keeping everything in place like a bubble.

It is designed to give the cell structure, shape, and stability. It is also a very flexible structure, so the cell can move freely. It is designed both to regulate the movement of nutrients and oxygen into the interior of the cell and to safely and rapidly remove waste from within the cell. It is semipermeable, meaning that some compounds can naturally diffuse across it to gain access to the internal environment of the cell (the ones with that ability are generally small, simple compounds).

There are, however, a huge array of different things that can affect the functioning of our cells. Most of these cannot freely enter the cell. Some that actually need to enter the cell to instigate their activities and stimulate changes require facilities for what is known as "active transport." This is where a certain structure—a specific transport mechanism if you will—in the cell membrane can actually bind to the substance in question and pull it in. These transport systems are selective. They recognize the specific substance that they need to look after and that alone. This stops other potentially dangerous substances using the structures to gain entry to the cell at random.

There is a third category of things that can influence what happens within our cells: these compounds do not need to enter the cell physically in order to instigate their activity upon it. These compounds actually interact with the cells and cause a whole cascade of chemical reactions to take place within it, without even having physically to enter it to do so. These compounds, such as hormones, need ...

CELL RECEPTORS

Cell receptors are specialized structures that are built into the cell membrane. They both project out into the extracellular (outside the cell) environment and into the intracellular (inside the cell) environment, too. Their role is to carry signals and messages that are sent from the outside, in order to stimulate changes inside the cell. They only bind to specific types of molecule. These may be hormones, neurotransmitters (chemicals that carry messages throughout the nervous system), cytokines (proteins that send specific commands to cells, often used by the immune system), and compounds that regulate tissue growth.

Receptors don't just attach to any old communication compound. There are as many different receptors as there are compounds, and each is uniquely designed. It could be viewed as a lock-and-key system. Specific receptors can be likened to a lock that is a specific shape that can fit a specific key. Hormones, neurotransmitters, cytokines, and growth factors are the key that will fit the specific lock, and are known as a ligand (the specific object that fits a receptor and instigates a response). When the ligand binds with the receptor, the receptor will set in motion a series of chemical responses inside the cell, that vary from a simple change through to an incredibly complex daisy chain of reactions, in order to bring about changes in the behavior, growth, or metabolism of the cell. Receptors and hormones are going to be cropping up a lot in this book. Especially the hormone insulin and its receptor!

ORGANELLES

Once we go into the cell, we find that there are a huge range of structures in there to perform every conceivable reaction necessary for life. There are many organelles, most that we don't need to worry a great deal about here, but I will give you a little overview. Probably the most well-known of the organelles is the nucleus. This is the control center of our cells and is the thing that is portrayed as a little dot or sphere in the center of pictures and diagrams of cells (and that's a pretty fair representation of the truth). The nucleus is where our DNA is found.

Other organelles are involved in facilitating chemical reactions, modifying, assembling, and storing vital metabolic substances, and generally controlling a massive range of functions and events that take place in our cells during every moment of every day.

Probably the most important in terms of what we are discussing here is an organelle called the mitochondria. This is a small sausage-shape structure that is the energy factory of our cells. This is really the final place where food becomes energy, or at least gives rise to the energy that our cells use to function. The mitochondria has an unique double-layered structure that is almost like a sac within a sac. Imagine one sac with many folds in it, placed inside another smooth sac. This curious double layering is vital to the mitochondria's function and is there to allow two different stages of chemical reactions to take place in order for our cells to make the energy we need.

HOW CELLS MAKE ENERGY

This is the next important area for us to cover. It will also help drive some of the key points home a little later on and just give you a background for better understanding of the whole process. Things can get a little complicated, but don't worry too much. I'm just trying to give you the broadest picture I can. There's no test at the end. Honest!

Everyone knows that the food we eat is where our energy comes from. But it obviously has to go through many changes in order to be utilized. Cells require a lot of energy. The amount of complex chemical reactions that they undertake constantly is really rather mind-boggling. We are talking literally hundreds of thousands of things going on inside the cells and tissues of our body every second. This life-giving activity requires energy, and lots of it, too.

I will go into greater detail later about how food is digested and how the energy is released from foods, but for now, what we need to know is that cells' first choice of energy to run on is glucose. We can run very effectively on fats, too ... more on that later. When we eat a meal, glucose, to a greater or lesser extent, will enter into the bloodstream and become available to the body. When glucose is available following a meal, the hormone insulin gets released from the pancreas and lets all our cells know that glucose is here and it is ready to use. Insulin then binds to its receptor and tells cells to take in glucose ... and do it quickly. Glucose transporters open and in comes the glucose. Once inside the cells, the glucose needs to be put to use. Unfortunately, it isn't as simple as cells simply running off glucose, more work needs to be done. Glucose needs to be converted into something called ATP (Adenosine Triphosphate). This is what gives the cell the energy it needs. It is the actual energy currency of the cell.

ATP has a specific structure. It consists of a substance called adenosine that is bound to three phosphates (again, don't get too worried about the details, just the general concept). These are held together by very high-energy chemical bonds. When needed, one of the three phosphates can be chopped off to release the high energy found in these bonds to power chemical reactions within the cell. What's left behind is something called ADP (Adenosine Diphosphate). Tri = 3, Di = 2; before it was a *Tri*phosphate then, after one of the phosphates has been removed, it becomes a *Di*phosphate. This has to then have another phosphate attached to it, returning it to the triphosphate and restoring that huge amount of energy in the bond. This takes place in the mitochondria, the organelle described on the previous page.

Sugars and fats contain many high-energy bonds. If you recall, the mitochondria is composed of a sac within a sac. In the space between the two sacs, these fuel substances (glucose and fats) are broken apart to release the high energy in them, as electrons.

These electrons then activate pumps that force hydrogen across into the inner sac. These hydrogens in turn then move through something called ATP Synthase, and generate enough energy to bind a new phosphate on to the ADP.

OK, I know this sounds a little bit geeky and complex and you don't need to know it inside out. The point I want to drive home is that cells respond to external signaling that lets them know that fuel is available. This fuel goes through a series of reactions that power our cells. That's it in a nutshell.

Phew. Hopefully that is the hard part over. It will all be worth it, I promise: these key points will put some of the later information into context for you.

DIGESTION OF FOOD AND ABSORPTION OF NUTRIENTS

So you have an idea of how your cells make energy and the mechanisms they use to know that there is fuel available for them. So, the next step is to look at the digestive processes that liberate this energy, and how things are regulated, before we get onto looking at what happens when things begin to go wrong and what you can do to change your diet today to begin to benefit your health and improve or manage your diabetes. This is one area where we truly need to go into a little bit of depth and detail.

Once you really understand this area, one of the key dietary strategies, food combining (which is in fact incredibly simple in practice) will make complete sense to you, and you will understand its impact in managing your diabetes and begin to get a good grasp on how important this is.

CARBOHYDRATES AND THEIR DIGESTION

Carbohydrates are probably the most important group of nutrients for you to understand when it comes to diabetes. They come in all shapes and sizes and really do consist of the good, the bad, and the ugly. The bottom line, though, is that they are digested to release their simplest components: sugars!

The carbohydrates that we consume vary in terms of their structures and complexity. Some carbohydrate-rich foods are made up of a lot of fiber, with very few actually digestible elements that can give us sugars for absorption. These are the higher fiber foods such as grains, and beans, and so on. Others are very simple, meaning that they are either sugars that are ready or almost-ready for immediate utilization, or that they are foods that require very little digestive effort in order for your body to liberate their sugars from them: think candies, or white bread.

The more complex carbohydrates are called polysaccharides, meaning they are a very complex bundle of lots of sugars bound together (poly = many; saccharide = sugar). The more simple variety tend to come in the form of disaccharides, while the simplest of all are the monosaccharides, such as glucose. These distinctions will become drastically important later on. Being carb-wise will be one of the most important factors for safeguarding your future health.

MOUTH

Carbohydrate digestion starts almost immediately in the mouth. When we chew a food, we secrete saliva. This serves two purposes. Firstly, it softens the food and lubricates it in order to make it easier to swallow. Secondly, saliva contains an enzyme called salivary amylase. This enzyme kick-starts the first steps of carbohydrate digestion, beginning to break starches down into disaccharides (simpler sugar molecules). You may have noticed that when you chew a baked potato, you detect a sweetness from it pretty quickly.

SIMPLE AND COMPLEX SUGARS

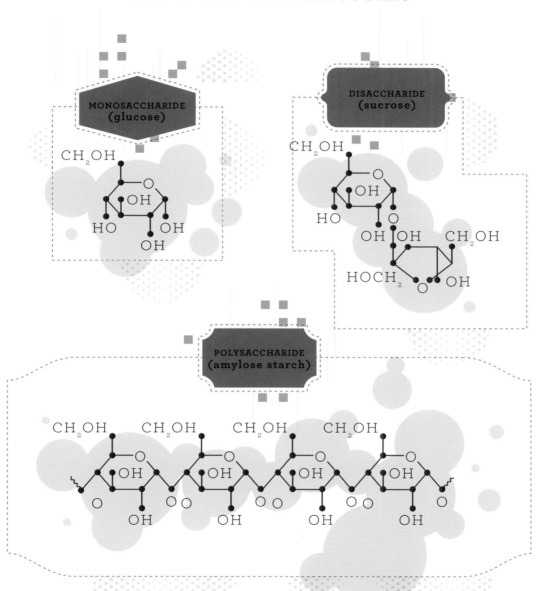

That taste is the simpler sugars being released by salivary amylase. This enzyme by no means liberates all of the sugars, it merely begins the process, to make things a little easier later on.

STOMACH

Very little digestion of carbohydrate takes place in the stomach. The stomach is an acidic environment and there are no enzymes present to break the complex bonds of polysaccharides. But stomach acid can break the disaccharide sucrose (the granulated stuff you put in your tea) into the monosaccharides fructose and glucose. Depending on the composition of a meal, foodstuffs can stay in the stomach for up to six hours (though the average is three or four). Food will leave in little dribs and drabs, rather than in a sudden flood. (This is going to be a vital thing to think about later on in this book, so I want you to remember this little nugget; it is an important justification for thinking about meal composition.) As soon as the food leaves the stomach, it enters the small intestine, where carbohydrate digestion continues.

SMALL INTESTINE

Once food leaves the stomach, it enters the small intestine. At this stage the pancreas releases an array of enzymes, including pancreatic amylase (the rock-hard big brother of salivary amylase), which splits polysaccharides (depending on composition) into disaccharides: sucrose, lactose, and maltose being most common.

As these travel through the small intestine, the intestinal walls secrete enzymes called sucrase, lactase, and maltase that split these disaccharides into their monosaccharide components, which are then ready for absorption.

The rate at which food enters the small intestine, the meal composition, as well as the complexity of the carbohydrates, will all be vitally important factors to consider later on. I know I keep saying that, but with good reason. All will become clear!

LARGE INTESTINE

Some of the more complex fibrous carbohydrates don't get degraded too much by pancreatic enzymes and intestinal secretions. They are pretty tough customers and are resilient to much of the digestive onslaught. This is partly why they are so beneficial to health. Some of them do get broken down to a certain extent in the large intestine, by another unique method.

The large intestine is the home to a massive array of bacterial life. You have heard of probiotics, right? Those little bugs that come in little funky yogurt drinks, or capsules. Well, these are a small cross-section of the population of bacteria that live in our digestive system. These bugs play a vast array of important roles, but one of the things that they can do is ferment and break down certain complex carbohydrates. Some of the complex polysaccharides will ferment and break down into smaller components, releasing some sugars. They also release a range of fatlike compounds that can offer some localized repair to the digestive tract tissue.

Once carbohydrates have been digested and broken down into their smallest components, they are sent into the bloodstream as glucose ready for use. Once the body has taken as much as it needs, excess glucose is stored as glycogen (the storage form of glucose) in our liver and muscles, as a type of "rainy day fund" for use later on.

PROTEINS AND FATS AND THEIR DIGESTION

OK, so it is probably less necessary to know the ins and outs of the digestion of these two macronutrients for the needs of this book, but a little overview will be useful to strengthen the understanding of some of the concepts that appear later on.

STOMACH

The stomach is perfectly geared up for protein digestion. It is a highly acidic environment. The hydrochloric acid in the stomach combines with something called pepsinogen to form pepsin, which begins to break the bonds that hold the protein together. Some of the more simple proteins can begin to be broken into their individual amino acids (the building blocks that combine to make proteins) at this stage. Most, however, have to move onto the small intestine to be broken down.

Fats are only marginally affected by stomach secretions. Enzymes called lipases begin to break fats down to a degree but, in the most part, fat digestion takes place within the small intestine.

Both proteins and fats cause the stomach to work quite hard to break them down and so they can stay in the stomach for some time. Their presence slows down the movement of food from the stomach to the intestine (in comparison to more simply composed meals), which is an important point to remember. When you eat a meal that has good-quality protein and fat sources in it, their complexity means that the food will leave the stomach at a slower rate.

SMALL INTESTINE

Once the food has left the stomach (which can really take some time with high-quality proteins and fiber), protein digestion is undertaken by two enzymes: trypsin and chymotrypsin. These enzymes break proteins down into their individual building blocks: amino acids. These are sent into circulation. Some will go straight to specific tissues, but most will be sent to the liver where they are strung together in sequence to make specific proteins that are needed for the body.

Fat digestion really happens predominantly in the small intestine. Bile that is secreted into the small intestine from the gall bladder breaks large globules of fat into smaller droplets that are easier for the body to deal with. The smaller they are, the more surface area they have and the more enzymes can work on them. Once these smaller droplets are formed, lipases act on them and break them down into small particles that are ready for absorption.

BLOOD SUGAR REGULATION

So, now we have got a bit of an idea about how food is digested to give us fuel, how our cells use this fuel, and how they respond to signaling in order to do this, we are ready for the next stage. This is where the rubber really hits the road. This is the bit that will bring everything together. This is (drum roll, please): blood sugar regulation and management.

Your blood sugar is the amount of glucose in circulation that is available for cells to use as a fuel source for turning into ATP, or the amount that is available for storage as glycogen. It basically is the measure of how much glucose is in your blood at any one time. Glucose is the primary source of fuel for the body, although under certain conditions we can use fatty acids quite happily. Because of this, you would think that the more blood sugar we have kicking around, the better it would be for us and the more energy we would be making. Well, sadly, things are never that simple in the body.

If we have too little sugar in the bloodstream, we have a problem. But, if we have too much sugar in the bloodstream, we are in trouble then, too! Too much or too little can literally be life threatening. If our blood sugar gets too low, in the short term we can become lethargic, irritable, and suffer impaired mental faculties. If this gets severe, as in a state of starvation, we can get paranoid, aggressive, eventually lose consciousness, and—if it's not addressed—even die. On the other hand, if blood sugar levels get too high for too long, then we can develop severe damage to the eyes, kidneys, nervous system, and cardiovascular system (there will be more detail on all of this later).

Because of this potentially grim picture if things get out of balance, we have mechanisms in place that can accurately control our blood sugar levels. So what are normal levels? Well, in healthy individuals, blood sugar sits at around 4.0–5.9mmol/l at a fasting level (ie having not eaten for a time). Following a meal, healthy blood sugar levels should remain below 7.8mmol/l. There is, of course, variation between individuals, while the food that we eat at a meal can really affect the levels too, as some foods can overload the system, where others supply glucose at an even trickle.

LOW BLOOD SUGAR

Let's start with a quick look at what happens when blood sugar levels get low. Low blood sugar will massively affect the performance of your body on every conceivable level, so we really cannot afford to let blood sugar dip very low at all, or we are in trouble. In light of this, the body has a very effective way of having a backup. Some of the sugar that enters the body from a meal will be put into storage. The body is like the serial saver that always banks 10 percent of their salary, storing some glucose in the form of glycogen, scurried away into the emergency fund.

If your blood sugar levels dip a bit too low, a group of cells in our pancreas called alpha cells release a hormone called glucagon. This quickly stimulates the release and then the conversion of glycogen —stored in the liver and muscles—back into glucose, which is released steadily into the bloodstream.

However, these stores are pretty important and your body won't simply let you run on reserves without topping them back off again; you have obviously had to dip into reserves for good reason. So, at the same time, there will be a stimulation of appetite, a signal for you to top yourself off.

HIGH BLOOD SUGAR

The most relevant area of blood sugar regulation in the context of this book, however, is what happens when blood sugar begins to rise. This rise occurs as simple sugars are liberated from the foods that we eat and begin to get absorbed into general circulation. When this happens and the blood sugar levels begins to rise, a different group of cells in the pancreas start to spring into action.

"One in four kids has either prediabetes or diabetes. What I like to call diabesity. How did this happen?"

DR. MARK HYMAN

These are the beta cells. It is these cells that are defective, due to damage by the immune system, in type-1 diabetes, which causes sufferers to have to inject themselves with insulin daily. When the beta cells spur into action, they start to secrete the hormone insulin, the most powerful regulator of metabolism in our body.

When released, insulin will move through the body rapidly and bind to a specific type of cell receptor (remember those structures that connect the insides of the cell to the outer environment), unsurprisingly called the insulin receptor. Upon binding to the receptor, insulin will instigate several key functions. The first one is a response that opens the flood gates in the walls of the cell (otherwise known as glucose transporters) and makes cells begin to take up glucose rapidly. In most situations, this system is absolutely adequate and works with pinpoint accuracy. We have the perfect balance in the body between glucose coming in from dietary sources, glucose being stored as glycogen, and insulin stimulating an increased glucose uptake by our cells.

However, this isn't always the case and—when abused—this system can eventually go wrong and break down. For example, when blood sugar is very high for a long time, our cells start to get full. They do, after all, only have a finite capacity for taking up glucose in a single sitting. If this is the case, blood sugar stays high, but the body still has to get rid of it. Blood sugar levels that stay so high are life threatening, so we have another mechanism in place that can deal with them. This is a chemical reaction: lipogenesis. I'm going to swerve all the real geeky information for now, though we will revisit it later. The short version is that the quickest way to deal with the excess sugar is to turn it into something else: fat! It is transformed into types of fatty substances known as triglycerides, which can be sent to our adipose tissue (body fat) for storage.

Insulin fuels this conversion and it also opens the gateway into adipocytes (the cells that make up our body fat), allowing the triglycerides to enter. This can not only cause us to gain weight, but can be devastating to the health of the cardiovascular system. Anyone that has read my book (*Eat Your Way to a Healthy Heart*) will be familiar with this process.

THE PANCREAS

The pancreas is a real key in the diabetes picture, so it would be rude not to talk about it a bit! It is a small organ that sits behind the stomach and releases substances into the body that deliver specific functions. These could be enzymes that aid digestion, or the all-important hormone insulin.

Within the pancreas there is a specialized area called the islets of Langerhans. This is a cluster of cells that manufacture hormones. One group of cells within the islets of Langerhans, called the beta cells, manufacture, store, and release upon demand the hormone insulin, to signal to cells to take up glucose. In type-1 diabetes, it is believed that the immune system attacks these beta cells at a very young age, damaging them and rendering them useless. This causes the patient to have to inject insulin every day, as the beta cells are unable to do their job.

WHEN THINGS GO WRONG: THE DISEASE PROCESSES OF DIABETES

A big part of my whole ethos is that we should be educated and empowered when it comes to our health, so we can do our best to be sitting in the driver's seat. Having a bit of an overview of what is happening in terms of your own health puts you in a better position to understand how to take the right action. I believe that we should be as informed as possible about our own health. So, here is a bit of a guide to how things go wrong in type-2 diabetes, before we move onto discuss what can be done to address the issue.

INSULIN RESISTANCE

Insulin resistance is essentially the first stage in the many processes that are creating and exacerbating the metabolic chaos that is afflicting the modern Western world.

In the last couple of decades we have seen massive increases in many chronic degenerative diseases and modern medicine is really struggling to manage them successfully. Many of these diseases are centered around key metabolic processes: cardiovascular disease, diabetes, and so on.

These are on the increase on a drastic scale. I'd go as far as to say that they are now running at epidemic proportions in the Western world. Just look at the numbers. This truly isn't an exaggeration.

One element that has been seen as a major link between these metabolic issues is insulin resistance: the series of events that cause our cells to stop listening to the insulin that we produce. So, what causes this? Well, before we get on to the biggest and main cause, there certainly can be a genetic factor at play here. While in almost 90 percent of cases it is due to lifestyle, genetic tendencies do exist. Some people do show a greater genetic susceptibility toward insulin resistance, regardless of any other influences, such as diet and lifestyle. However, this is only in a *very* small number of cases.

On the whole, insulin resistance arises almost totally because of lifestyle factors, the biggest of those being—as we are beginning to see—the food that we eat!

WHAT CAUSES INSULIN RESISTANCE?

When we eat, the food is broken down by digestion into its constituent parts: macronutrients (proteins, fats, and carbohydrates) and micronutrients (vitamins, minerals, trace elements, and so on), which then go on to enter the bloodstream following absorption and are shipped around to different places to do different jobs.

When sugars from our diet enter the bloodstream, our body releases the hormone insulin in response. It is the job of insulin to bind to specialized insulin receptors built into our cells. When insulin binds to these receptors, it causes a response that opens up "doorways" in the cell that allow glucose to enter, so it can be utilized as energy.

When we consume foods that are whole and complex and don't contain large amounts of simple sugars, this series of events takes place consistently, evenly, and painlessly. However, when we consume foods that release their sugars very quickly, or that are a concentrated source of simple sugars, we basically start to carpet-bomb the bloodstream with sugar. This causes our bodies to respond by pumping out higher levels of insulin. Every now and again, this is not a problem, such as having a piece of chocolate once in a while. But when it goes on for weeks, months, years, decades, things can begin to go seriously wrong.

Consistently excessive levels of insulin soon start to raise the suspicions of the cells it is communicating with. It's almost like the boy that cried wolf. When insulin is consistently being kicked out of the beta cells in the pancreas in response to the floods of blood sugar, the cells will eventually begin to think that something is up. They will start to question what is going on with insulin and whether it really knows what on earth it is doing.

THE GLUCOSE AND INSULIN RELATIONSHIP

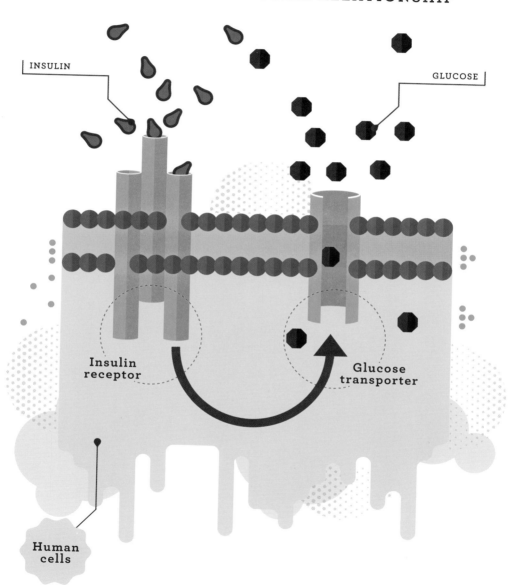

INSULIN

GLUCOSE

Insulin
receptor

Glucose
transporter

Human
cells

When this occurs, the cell receptor basically starts to think that insulin is getting a little too carried away with itself and feels it is best ignored. So, the receptor ignores insulin, it basically becomes less receptive to the signal that insulin is sending out.

Now, being something of a persistent character, insulin doesn't take "no" for an answer. With reduced cellular response to insulin, there is a reflex increase in production of insulin from the beta cells of the pancreas. As far as they are concerned, there isn't enough insulin out there to get its message heard. This increased production can work for a while but, before long, the insulin receptors really do dig their heels in and become even more resistant to insulin. Strangely enough, this state is called insulin resistance! It is a situation which some would say is prediabetic. I certainly agree that, unchecked, it sets the stage for type-2 diabetes. At this point, blood glucose levels start to rise notably as cells become less receptive and we begin to see medical signs of a state called hyperglycemia: consistently elevated blood glucose.

INSULIN RESISTANCE AND OBESITY

However, diabetes is only one outcome of insulin resistance; the worst-case scenario that arises after prolonged, untreated insulin resistance. There is an epidemic of metabolic chaos sweeping the Western world.

This is manifesting in what is termed "metabolic syndrome." It is a cluster of several symptoms, but essentially all are linked to insulin resistance. When insulin levels are raised for long enough, one of the first clinical manifestations we would be aware of is abdominal obesity. This is the incredibly hard-to-shift fat that collects around the middle. You know the stuff. It is the fat that no amount of hours on the treadmill will shift and no diet—so far—has even touched.

There are two main reasons for this occurring when we have insulin resistance issues. Firstly, if insulin is higher, that generally means blood sugar is higher, and blood sugar that is too high must be dealt with. In normal circumstances, this excess of sugar would be taken up by cells and put to use in the manufacture of energy. However, when cells are resistant to insulin, their capacity to take in glucose is restricted. This leads to an excess of glucose that needs to be shifted! So, what happens next is a reaction called lipogenesis where, in short, the sugar gets converted into fats.

These fats, known as triglycerides, are much easier to be got rid of, as they are able to be carried away and stored in our adipose tissue (body fat). Insulin opens the gates within adipocytes (fat cells) to let these fatty acids in. What happens in normal situations is that these fatty acids will go into fat cells for storage but, when insulin levels fall, they can freely flow back out again and be used by the body as energy.

Unfortunately, when insulin is high it becomes like a one-way flow of traffic, with fatty acids collecting in the adipocytes (fat cells) and insulin keeping them from coming back out again. Before long, this becomes a pattern of weight gain and no amount of exercise will get rid of it. Get insulin under control, on the other hand, and you will see this stubborn fat disappearing for the first time.

INSULIN RESISTANCE, INCREASED CHOLESTEROL, AND HIGH BLOOD PRESSURE

The next clinical manifestation that may be seen during insulin resistance / metabolic syndrome is an increase in cholesterol and blood fats. In light of what has just been said, this should be quite a logical thing. When sugar turns into triglycerides, it is carried to the adipose tissue through the general circulation, so blood fats go up. This causes an increase in the production of the body's fat transport system: the lipoproteins. These are specialized carriers that ferry fats and cholesterol around the body. When triglycerides go up, the first thing that happens is the body produces more of something called VLDL or Very Low Density Lipoprotein. This gets degraded by various enzymes and becomes LDL.

Both VLDL and LDL are considered atherogenic, which means they are thought to play a role in the instigation of heart disease. They are believed to be susceptible to oxidation, causing localized inflammation which can damage the vessel walls. They are also believed to be more capable, under the right circumstances, of penetrating the walls of the blood vessels, where they instigate the beginnings of a plaque (a buildup of fatty material). Another major complication of insulin resistance is high blood pressure. This may be due to altered kidney function, or it could be due to influences on the endothelium, affecting vascular dynamics. The exact link isn't clear, but we know it is there.

So in essence, you may know someone, or you yourself, may have the triad of issues that are considered metabolic syndrome: type-2 diabetes / prediabetes, high LDL cholesterol, and high blood pressure. These are all caused—or at least exacerbated—by a breakdown of our body's ability to handle simple sugars and the chain of events that unfold as a result of this.

BETA CELL DYSFUNCTION

The next step in the progression from insulin resistance to full-blown type-2 diabetes, when this occurs, is a dysfunction of the beta cells in the pancreas. As we have seen earlier in the book, beta cells are the specialized cells found in an area of the pancreas called the islets of Langerhans. Their job is to store and release insulin. After prolonged states of insulin resistance and hyperglycemia, in most cases, the next step is an impairment in the function of the beta cells. There is a progressive reduction in the amount of insulin they secrete. There is still much discussion and research around why this may be the case. The most likely scenarios at present are glucotoxicity and elevation of free fatty acids.

When blood glucose levels are consistently high and insulin is failing to induce a cellular response (insulin resistance), the level of glucose can become toxic. This is a state called glucotoxicity and can cause untold damage. In the beta cells it is believed that glucotoxicity can cause mitochondrial dysfunction, increase oxidative stress, and ultimately lead to apoptosis: cell death! As we have also seen, elevated blood glucose can lead to an increase in fatty acids in the blood. This increase in free fatty acids is also believed to instigate changes in the cell that lead to apoptosis. At this stage of beta cell dysfunction, individuals may be advised by their physician that they need to inject themselves with insulin. They are essentially at the same place as a type-1 diabetic.

HOW TYPE-2 DIABETES AND PREDIABETES ARE DIAGNOSED

There are several tests that can be used when diagnosing diabetes. Some give crude results, while others are really more specific.

URINE TESTING

Urine tests are often used when you go to your physician for a general checkup. It is often the case that if you go to the physician to get an idea of your general health at certain stages of life, they will give you a blood test that checks for cardiovascular disease markers such as cholesterol levels, check your blood pressure, and also test a urine sample for glucose. Urine doesn't usually contain glucose, but if blood glucose levels get particularly high, it can begin to escape via the kidneys and exit the body via the urine. The problem with this test, however, is that it just gives a suggestion that there may be a problem, rather than anything specific. It gives the clinician the impetus to do more testing and is seen as a noninvasive starting point. It may well be the case that the patient is diabetic or prediabetic, or there may be a very simple benign transient cause for this rise in glucose, such as an Easter egg-eating marathon! It can alert practitioners to a potential problem in an unthreatening and easy way, but doesn't really tell them much more than there is a lot of glucose present currently.

ORAL GLUCOSE TOLERANCE TEST

Another relatively common test is the oral glucose tolerance test. This basically measures how the body deals with glucose. The patient is asked to fast for eight to 12 hours before the test. Upon arrival they have a base sample of blood taken. This shows glucose levels following a period of fasting. In healthy individuals, the base level of glucose should be less than 6.1mmol/L. A level of above 7.0mmol/L is believed to confirm a diagnosis of diabetes.

They are then given a standard dose of glucose. After two hours, a further blood sample is taken to measure the amount of glucose present in the blood, in order to determine how effectively the body has dealt with it. In a healthy individual, blood glucose two hours after consuming the standardized dose should be below 7.8mmol/L. A level of between 7.8mmol/L and 11.1mmol/L indicates an impaired glucose tolerance. A level above 11.1mmol/L again is diagnostic of diabetes.

GLYCATED HEMOGLOBIN / HBA1C

There is one test that has now become a bit of a benchmark. It is thought that this test gives the best long-term picture of an individual's glucose levels. This is measuring the level of glycated hemoglobin, a type of hemoglobin that is formed upon exposure to glucose. Glycation is basically a binding between a protein and a sugar, in this case hemoglobin and glucose. It is normal to find some glycated hemoglobin, but the longer blood glucose remains elevated the higher the amount. So, individuals that are at the point where they are getting notably insulin resistant and whose blood glucose levels are getting and staying very high will have a far higher level of glycated hemoglobin. If this number is higher, then the individual would have had raised glucose for longer, giving a more accurate indication that there are pathological changes rather than transient fluctuations. Normal healthy individuals should have a level of 5.7 percent or lower. A level of up to 6.4 percent is considered to show insulin resistance or prediabetic stages. A reading of above 6.5 percent is believed to be indicative of diabetes.

THE ROLE OF NUTRITION IN THE MANAGEMENT AND PREVENTION OF DIABETES AND INSULIN RESISTANCE

The information you have just read does offer a rather gloomy picture for our health. Still to this day, the conventional wisdom is that type-2 diabetes cannot be reversed and that once you have it, you have it for life. It is certainly true that type-1 diabetes is irreversible, but can absolutely be effectively improved by the right approach to diet. Type-2, on the other hand, is a different story. In spite of the less optimistic conventional stance, there is a *vast* evidence base to show that changes in diet and lifestyle can offer massive improvements in individual's symptoms and in clinical markers of the disease. There are huge numbers of documented cases of individuals reversing their condition, but I couldn't possibly say that it is a guarantee, that it will definitely be the case for you.

What I will say with absolute certainty is that, if you implement these changes, you will get huge benefits to your condition. Of this I assure you.

In type-2 diabetes, there can be several manifestations of the condition. Some individuals will just be in a state where they are insulin resistant, in that their cells just aren't responsive to insulin signaling. This is the early stages, the precarious border between prediabetes and full-blown type-2 diabetes. Others, on the other hand, as we have seen above—mostly those that have had the condition for some time—will get dysfunction of the pancreas, where it no longer makes sufficient insulin (in response to the consistently elevated level that starts the condition off). It is my personal belief that individuals in the first category, those where severe insulin resistance is their main pathological factor, or those who have just moved into full-blown type-2, are the ones who are the most likely to see reversal of the condition.

But it is certain that everyone will benefit to some degree when they make the right dietary changes. It is completely logical and really a no-brainer. I do also believe that providing you don't have any complications associated with your type-2 diabetes (which *must* be dealt with by the relevant drugs from your physician, without question), then the dietary changes and strategies I suggest, providing you *stick to them for life*, will be the most suitable long-term intervention for you.

LEARN TO REACH FOR LOW-GLYCEMIC FOODS

Learning the glycemic value of foods will be one of the key tools that will help you to shape your diet for life and will soon become second nature to you.

It can be a little complex if you really delve deep, but you will soon start to see a pattern forming and before long it will be easy to know what foods are what and, trust me, you will end up making your choices and putting together meals almost on autopilot.

There are several terms that are frequently used in the health and diet worlds that have the word glycemic in them, and all are important. The first one—and one that is probably familiar to most people—is the glycemic index (GI). This is a measure of how quickly blood sugar levels go up after eating a certain food. It is basically a measure of how the carbohydrates in a certain food will affect your blood sugar. It gives you this value in comparison to the rate at which pure glucose would send blood sugar up. This is a fairly useful starting point as it gives you an indication as to which foods are most likely to be problematic for you. But, it doesn't give you the full picture.

A further extension of this is something called the glycemic load (GL). This measurement takes the glycemic index, then combines that with the actual amount of usable carbohydrate that is in a portion of the given food. A food could have a very high-GI carbohydrate in it, but a portion of that food may actually have

FOOD	GLYCEMIC INDEX	SERVING SIZE	GLYCEMIC LOAD
Sweet foods			
Honey	87	2 Tbsp	17.9
Table sugar	68	2 tsp	7
Jam	51	2 Tbsp	10.1
Cereal & Bread			
Corn flakes	92	28g	21.1
Rice Krispies	82	33g	23
Special K	69	31g	14.5
Oatmeal	58	117g	6.4
French bread	95	64g (1 slice)	29.5
White loaf	70	25g (1 slice)	8.4
Whole-wheat loaf	70	28g (1 slice)	7.7
Pumpernickel bread	41	26g (1 slice)	4.5
Drinks (soft)			
Orange juice	57	250ml	14.25
Cranberry juice	68	250ml	24.5
Apple juice	41	250ml	11.9
Cola	63	370ml (can)	25.2
Legumes			
Baked beans	48	253g	18.2
Chickpeas	31	240g	13.3
Kidney beans	27	256g	7
Lentils (green)	29	198g	7
Soybeans	20	172g	1.4
Peanuts	13	146g	1.6
Vegetables			
Potato	104	213g	36.4
Parsnip	97	78g	11.6
Carrot	92	15g	1
Beet	64	246g	9.6
Sweet potato	51	136g	16.8
Peas	48	72g	3.4
Fruit			
Watermelon	72	152g	7.2
Pineapple	66	155g	11.9
Apples	39	138g (1 medium)	6.2
Banana	51	118g	12.2
Plums	24	66g	1.7
Grapes	43	92g	6.5
Pears	33	166g	6.9
Peaches	28	98g	2.2

The chart, left, is obviously not even close to an exhaustive list. If it was, I would create a book of a size that would make Tolkien feel inadequate, and it would be so dull it would anesthetize the most hardened of insomniacs! These books do exist —and please be my guest and grab one—but you really don't need it. This table is simply to illustrate my big key points: choose foods that are in their whole state (brown over white, minimally processed); make sure they have plenty of fiber (pumpernickel bread or lentils, for example); and you will be choosing foods that by default have a very low glycemic impact indeed. Follow this trend, along with the correct food-combining techniques, and you will have it nailed for life. A little note about proteins such as meat and fish ... luckily these sit at a big fat zero, so go nuts and make them the stars of the show.

very little usable total carbohydrate in it, thus having a low glycemic load. That's not as complicated as it sounds. Let's use watermelon as an example. The carbohydrates in watermelon have a glycemic index of 72 (wow! Pure glucose is 100) which is an incredibly high value. However, a reasonable 3½oz (100g) portion of watermelon only has 5g of carbohydrate in it. That seems like less of a gargantuan number, doesn't it? So the calculation is: carbohydrate content in grams, multiplied by GI score, divided by 100. So, for watermelon: 5 x 72 / 100 = a GL score of 3.6. A food with a GL score of 20 is considered high.

OK, I know this may seem a bit like gobbledegook. Why does any of this matter? Well, these values basically tell you how the food that you eat is going to affect your blood sugar. Remember how we become less sensitive to insulin and what sets the stage for all of this? When we completely bombard our bodies with sugar on an ongoing basis, our insulin receptors start to gradually get less sensitive to insulin signaling and cells soon are unable to take up glucose to anywhere near the same extent that they were previously able to. The good news is that our bodies can bounce back very quickly when we give them an environment that allows it. So, if you are suffering from insulin resistance, prediabetes, or full-blown type-2 diabetes, the sooner you stop the bombardment of sugar, the better. Foods with lower GL values don't bombard the blood with sugar, instead, they drip-feed it in smaller amounts.

Smaller amounts of sugar, added to the bloodstream in small, manageable increments. Levels that don't require huge surges of insulin in order to deal with their sugar flood.

There are a few reasons why these types of foods will have more of a drip-feeding effect. Many tend to be of a more complex chemical structure, meaning that their available sugars are bound up in complex chemical bonds and require greater digestive effort to liberate them. Others require specific metabolic processes once absorbed, to liberate their energy. The important point is that these are the foods that you should be reaching for more. Why? Well, insulin resistance, given the chance, can bounce back pretty quickly. If you bring the glycemic impact of your whole diet down, then in time insulin receptors will start to believe what insulin is telling them again and become far more receptive to its influence. Over time your body will handle insulin properly, produce less of it, and manage blood sugar more effectively. It takes time and it takes discipline, but it is achievable.

CARB RESTRICTION AND GETTING CARB SMART

So you should now have some familiarity with the glycemic values of specific carbohydrate-rich foods. The next step is carb reduction and being carb smart. Don't panic, I'm not saying that you need to start doing the Atkins diet, but looking at your overall carbohydrate intake is of massive importance here, both for managing insulin resistance and diabetes and also for the complications that are associated with these conditions.

In general, in the Western world, our intake of carbohydrates has gone a little insane. We are consuming more of these foods than during any other period of history or our evolution. The pattern has changed to an alarming degree. This is due to a series of events that took place about 50 years ago, in the form of a very ill-informed public health campaign sparked in essence by just one man. His name was Ancel Keys.

Keys was an American physiologist with a strong interest in nutrition. He had been part of many dietary projects with the US government, including the development of the K-ration, a nutrient-dense bar that was given to American troops in the field to provide daily sustenance in a small portable unit. Keys had a theory that cardiovascular disease was caused by saturated fat and a nation's heart disease statistics would be a direct reflection of the amount of saturated fat that the population ate. So, he set about to prove it. To do this, he devised a study into the dietary habits of 22 countries. Each population's intake of saturated fat was compared against cardiovascular disease rates to search for the connection. Once the study was finished, the findings were published and, boy, did they prove the saturated fat and heart disease hypothesis perfectly. Case dismissed ... or was it? The only problem was that the data published was from only seven of the 22 countries. Hang on a second! Seven? What happened to the rest? Well, if the data from all 22 countries had been published, Keys's theory would have completely fallen apart. The data showed *absolutely no connection* at all between saturated fat intake and heart disease. But, Keys was an ambitious chap, and also had a lot of investors and backers who were certainly ... keen ... to see a specific result. So, data was selected that showed what Keys wanted to show. He used the data only from countries where a connection between saturated fats and heart disease could be found, that supported his beloved ideas, and completely threw out all the rest!

This outright fraud should have been massive news and a scandal, but no. Keys became a national hero and in no time at all was on the front cover of *Time* magazine.

Next, he was beginning to advise on government public health policy. When this happened, the US government soon developed a public health campaign that warned the American public to drastically reduce their intake of saturated fats and replace them with low-fat starchy foods such as bread, potatoes, and the like.

These were low-fat so *must* be "heart-healthy," right? Whoops! This message almost instantly shot across the Atlantic and became policy in the UK.

What happened next was the biggest public health mess of them all, and boy there have been a few! You can literally chart this on a graph when you look at disease patterns in populations from institutions such as the World Health Organization. We took on this message and our diets changed. Massively. It was breakfast cereal and margarine all around before you could say "death diet." As we moved increasingly toward the low-fat high-starch diet, our waistlines began to expand.

I am in my late 30s and I can remember being a child in the late 1970s and 1980s. Seeing someone overweight was really quite unusual. It wasn't unheard of, but it wasn't that often that you'd see someone that was struggling with their weight. But it was beginning to change. And people were starting to notice things changing. Diet clubs and the battle against the bulge began to sneak in, and it has been an absolute public health apocalypse. As the changes started taking hold, obesity, heart disease, metabolic syndrome, and type-2 diabetes soared. They went from a relatively small problem to epidemic proportions in a few generations.

Bearing in mind that we have been evolving for millions of years, a change that severe can *only* be the result of an environmental impact upon our physiology. It must be something *we* are doing or that *we* have changed, that is causing this. Our intake of starch and the wrong types of fats (I'm saving that nugget for a little later) went through the roof. This caused our blood sugar to go bananas, overloading our insulin system and unleashing metabolic chaos.

Constantly high blood sugar, coupled with poor fatty acid balance, meant that we were synthesizing fats and storing them around our collective midsections very quickly. Our insulin sensitivity went south and, at the same time, cardiovascular disease became the single biggest killer in the developed world.

This unnatural increase in carbohydrate intake, particularly intake of refined carbohydrates, has been killing us in our millions. You may not be directly aware of the amount of these foods that you are eating. But look at this picture and think if it sounds familiar. How many people would start the day with a bowl of cereal and maybe a slice or two of toast? Then at lunch time, it's not too extreme a statement to say that, for most, a weekday lunch would be a sandwich. An evening meal may be pasta, rice, potatoes, or a slice of bread to mop up the juices on the plate. Between meals there may be potato chips or a cereal bar, a cookie or a fruit smoothie. These are everyday patterns. When I work with clients and look at their food diaries, I see it consistently.

The sad thing is that we have been told for so long that these are healthy eating patterns and we believe we are doing the right thing. This is what truly saddens me most of all. I see so many people who truly want to make the right changes, but based on the poor public health information they have been given in the past, have been inadvertently destroying their health! When you look at it though, the amount of starchy foods and fast-release carbohydrates in our daily diets are getting to be at an extreme level.

So what *should* we do? Well, I would certainly encourage everyone to consider reducing their overall intake of starchy foods such as bread, pasta, rice, and potatoes. When you do want to include some of these types of foods—and there are indeed recipes in this book that use these types of ingredients (I want to lead you in the right direction slowly and comfortably rather than just force you into a massive dietary overhaul in one go)—then you need to be carb smart. This means choosing the best sources. So, you want some rice? Go for brown. Throw the white variety out of your pantry. You want a bit of bread? Have multigrain. These versions of the staple carbs in our diet are much more complex in their structures, take longer to digest, and release their energy (and affect blood sugar) more gradually.

"If we continue on the same trend, 10% of the world's population, around 592 million, will have diabetes by the year 2035."

INTERNATIONAL DIABETES FEDERATION

But, the key message and the thing I would really encourage you to do, is to reduce your overall consumption of these foods right across the board. Instead of nasty sugared breakfast cereals, opt for scrambled eggs or a frittata. If you absolutely must have a cereal-based breakfast, then oatmeal would be the best option, with a few nuts (for protein) on top.

Main meals should be centered around lean proteins, as many vegetables as you can possibly shoehorn in and generous helpings of good fats, such as olive oil, avocados, and nuts. Before you think this is a carb-free diet, I want to point out that vegetables are … carbohydrates. They are just carbohydrates that have a very low GL score so they give you a nice slow, sustained energy release, rather than simply napalming your bloodstream with a flood of sugar. These are the smartest carbs of them all and the ones that we should be filling up with as much as possible.

A little note about fruit: it is considered the perfect food by many and is seen as the ultimate healthy snack option. Well, I'm kind of 50:50 on this one. I think for people that don't have any blood sugar issues and are very active, fruit is great. But, for those of you that are suffering from blood sugar issues, I would be very cautious. I'd advise avoiding all the sweet juicy types and, if you really must have some, then apples and berries are going to be your best bet, as they have the lowest GL value.

MEAL COMPOSITION

After you have got to grips with choosing low glycemic foods and being carb smart, one of the best weapons you can have in your armory on a daily basis is to be aware of meal composition. The way in which you combine foods can have a huge impact on blood sugar levels, insulin response, and insulin sensitivity.

So, if the first part of the picture is choosing foods with the lowest GL values and keeping a curb on carbohydrate-dense foods, then the next part is how you eat them. The combination that foods are eaten in can affect their glycemic impact. If you recall, some foods, such as proteins, take a very long time to digest and stay in the stomach for much longer than other foodstuffs.

So, rule number one in every meal is: *look to see where your protein is coming from*. The protein in the meal will slow down the digestion and release of usable sugars from the meal considerably. The proteins require more digestive effort within the stomach, as hydrochloric acid does its thing to break the bonds. As we saw, very little in the way of carbohydrate digestion takes place in the stomach. So, a meal with a good protein content is going to leave the stomach much more slowly than would a simple carbohydrate meal. This basically releases the sugars from the meal into the bloodstream in a much more slow, sensible, and sustained fashion.

To take this process a step further, and bring down the glycemic impact of a meal even more, bring in a good source of fat with each meal. I'm not talking a pound of lard, but healthy fat sources such as olive and flax oil dressings, nut butters, avocados .... Fat slows gastric emptying, so this effect of drip-feeding blood sugar is enhanced even further.

Now, don't panic about fat. As we have seen above, the evidence that links fat and heart disease is complete nonsense and many studies since have backed this up further. Fats are an absolute vital nutrient for almost every body system. Cut them out of your diet at your peril.

Fats are essential for the manufacture of hormones, vitamin D synthesis, transporting fat-soluble nutrients, regulating the structure and function of cell membranes, regulating the inflammatory response, and many other metabolic functions.

Low-fat diets fail at keeping us healthy and anybody that has tried them long term will attest to that. Adding a good source of fat with each meal will have unforeseen benefits. Not only will it keep you feeling fuller and lower the glycemic response of the meal, but it will also help you to absorb the fat-soluble nutrients in the food as well as ensure that you get adequate intake of the vital essential fatty acids your body need each day. Fat. Get it in and don't be scared of it!

So, in practice, this is how we could put meals together. As I have mentioned previously, the ideal meal composition would be protein, vegetables, and fat. So an example of this would be a salmon salad with a bit of feta cheese and a nice olive oil dressing. It could be a baked chicken breast with steamed greens, roasted carrots, and a sauce made with soft cheese and dill, or even a good Sunday roast, minus the roasties ... OK, maybe a couple. Breakfast could be a frittata. If you wanted to have a cereal for breakfast, don't do it every day and, as I have said, go for an unsweetened oat-based cereal such as oatmeal or a clean (sugar-free) muesli. But, make sure you have protein and fat with it. This is an easy one. Sprinkling it with nuts and seeds gives you a good protein boost, plus a good lashing of important fats. Chicken with vegetable stir-fry and seedy quinoa. You get the picture, I am sure. The beautiful thing is that eating this way is a doddle and a joy, too. No weird exotic additions to your diet, merely being conscious of what is on your plate.

FATTY ACID COMPOSITION OF THE DIET

I have touched on the fact that fats are of drastic importance when it comes to our health. Our relationship with fat has gone dreadfully wrong and we are paying the price. Big time!

The problem we are facing started with the publication of Keys's very watered down study of 22 countries; remember, he only used the data from seven because their numbers proved his theory but, when all 22 were observed, the connection between fat and heart disease was nonexistent.

This farce caused an international public health campaign that drummed it into us that we need to avoid saturated fat like the plague and instead opt for more "heart-healthy" options such as sunflower oil, vegetable oil, corn oil, soy oil ...

"Rarely, type-2 diabetes develops without any readily identifiable predisposing factor. But in the great majority of cases, it is brought on by lifestyle activities ... most importantly dietary choices."

DR. DAVID PERLMUTTER

Why would this be a problem? Well, these types of oils are made up almost completely of omega 6 fatty acids. There are two essential fatty acids our bodies need to get from the diet and are vital to health. These are omega 3 and omega 6. So if they are important for health, what's the problem? Well, omega 6 is only needed in tiny amounts. When taken in these amounts it plays some very important roles in our body. Once we get past this level, this once beneficial compound becomes incredibly problematic.

Dietary fatty acids play many roles. One of their biggest is as metabolic building blocks for the production of an important group of communication compounds called prostaglandins.

Essential fatty acids are incorporated into our cell membranes and are liberated by an enzyme called phospholipase for use in daily metabolic processes, such as the formation of prostaglandins. These prostaglandins regulate several important responses in the body, including the inflammatory response. There are three types of prostaglandin: Series 1, Series 2, and Series 3. Series 1 is mildly anti-inflammatory, Series 2 is powerfully proinflammatory (ie it switches on and exacerbates inflammation), and Series 3 is powerfully anti-inflammatory.

Omega 6, when consumed at a level above our daily needs, gets converted into something called arachidonic acid. In turn, this is then converted into Series 2 prostaglandins, the powerfully proinflammatory variety. On average, the UK, is consuming 23 times more omega 6 than we need *per day*! The end result of this is that we are essentially force-feeding metabolic pathways that manufacture prostaglandins and our bodies' expression of the proinflammatory Series 2 goes into overdrive.

It's pretty logical what's going to happen here. This leads to a state of subclinical (ie not immediately obvious, such as your big toe swelling up), chronic (ongoing long-term) inflammation. In its most obvious manifestation, this can exacerbate inflammatory conditions such as arthritis and eczema.

But probably of more sinister consequence are the small, subtle changes that it makes within body tissues. Continual inflammation within tissues can lead to damage to them, such as that found in cardiovascular disease, when the blood vessel walls become damaged by inflammation and plaques then form. Inflammatory changes in tissues have also been linked to the changes that occur in the instigation of cancer.

The other thing this can do is affect cell receptor function. The fatty acid content of our cell membranes has a massive effect upon the cell and its functioning, and also upon the functioning of trans-membrane and membrane-bound structures. What one cellular structure is of great importance to us here? The insulin receptor. Our fatty acid intake *will* affect the performance of this, so we need to make sure it is correct.

So, on the flip side, the other big dietary fatty acid, one you have probably heard a great deal about: omega 3 fatty acids. These amazing fatty acids are almost an antidote to the above. There are three main types of omega 3 fatty acid: ALA, EPA, and DHA. As has been outlined, the essential fatty acids are the metabolic precursors to prostaglandins. EPA and DHA are actually metabolized to form Series 3 prostaglandins (EPA more so). These are the ones that are the most potently anti-inflammatory and an increase in their production can influence inflammatory events very quickly indeed. Consuming good quantities of omega 3 fatty acids encourages our body to produce more of the anti-inflammatory prostaglandins.

The benefits of omega 3 on heart health are well documented and have been studied widely for at least 20 years. However, in recent years we have found that omega 3 intake benefits other aspects of the metabolic disease storm that we are weathering. Increased omega 3 intake is associated with improved insulin production, utilization, and sensitivity. A study of 126 adults in rural British Columbia, Canada found that increased omega 3 intake was negatively associated with insulin resistance[1]. This is a population-based observation study and only shows associations rather than cause and effect, but some experimental studies have offered compelling support. A small experimental study conducted by Tsitouras et al in 2008 found that individuals who ate 1.5 lb (720 g) of fatty fish per week, and took 1 Tbsp (15 ml) of sardine oil daily, had greater insulin sensitivity after eight weeks than those who ate a control diet ②. There are many more of these small experimental studies and population-based studies around.

While more research is needed, it certainly looks like a pattern is emerging and, when viewed from a logical, physiological point of view, it makes sense. At the end of the day, the massive health benefits associated with increased omega 3 fatty acids across the board means that even if this observation proves to not hold true, there will be no harm to our health, only benefit.

So, as is becoming obvious, our fatty acid intake does become a bit of a balancing act. As you can see, omega 3 fatty acids are a pretty important part of the picture, while too much omega 6 can cause a problem. So it is vital to get the balance right. With the current trends arising from research, the recommendation now is to aim for a 2:1 ratio in favor of omega 3. That basically means that you need to be eating twice as much omega 3 than omega 6 in order to maximize the potential benefits, and counteract any negative effects of omega 6.

Thankfully this is pretty easy in practice. The first step is to avoid most vegetable oils like the plague. These are the apparently "heart-healthy" oils such as sunflower oil, corn oil, or generic vegetable oil. These are basically pure omega 6 and will send your levels rocketing up very fast.

In place of these oils there are two cooking oils to choose from. In most of my cooking I use olive oil. The dominant fatty acid in olive oil is something called oleic acid which comes into a third category: omega 9. Omega 9 fatty acids have zero influence on omega balance, so don't particularly present a problem at all.

The other oil I use to prepare food is coconut oil. This is best for high-temperature cooking as it is completely heat stable. Also the fatty acids found in there, medium chain triglycerides, are rapidly broken down and used as an energy source, so their impact on postprandial lipemia (elevation of blood fats after a meal) is minimal.

The next step in aiming for omega balance is to drastically cut back on processed foods. This is good advice for a million and one reasons but, in terms of omega balance, many processed foods use untold amounts of vegetable oils. They are very cheap and, for decades, food manufacturers have been under pressure to reduce saturated fat in foods, so have moved over to cheap vegetable oils as an alternative. Most ready meals, premade sauces, and so on will have a lot of omega 6 in them. Get back to basics, like we do in the recipes in this book and get into cooking your food from scratch as much as you can.

The second part of the picture is to up the omega 3. The first and most obvious place to start is by eating oily fish around three times per week. Then you could consider taking supplements as well. I personally take an omega 3 supplement that contains 750mg of EPA and 250mg of DHA twice daily. (If you are taking medications such as warfarin, or if you have recently had a heparin injection, please check with your physician first before using high-dose fish oil supplements as there is potential for interaction here.)

KEY HEALTHY INGREDIENTS FOR DIABETES

This isn't an exhaustive or specifically prescriptive list, rather a guide to some of the goodies that should fill your refrigerator and pantry on a regular basis. Thankfully you don't have to take a trip to any weird specialist stores in Outer Mongolia. These are all good, normal, healthy, and everyday foods that you will easily find anywhere.

BROWN RICE

OK, so grains consumed to high levels is a very very bad idea for diabetics! Even writing as a non-diabetic, I only eat them in very small amounts and not that often. However, in these smaller amounts—and when consumed with other key macronutrients in the right combinations—they will be a valuable part of the diet. Brown rice is a bit of a health food staple and one that, admittedly, does still have something of a hippyish image. But it is one of the best grain options, in my opinion. Firstly, it is a real slow burner. It has a seriously low glycemic response. It also has a very high fiber content that slows down its digestion and therefore sugar liberation. Finally, it has a really good hit of B vitamins, too.

BULGUR WHEAT

Similar to brown rice, bulgur wheat has a very high fiber content and really good levels of several B vitamins, plus some magnesium to boot! As well as a lovely nutty flavor and chewy texture. Bulgur wheat is a perfect alternative to rice and is particularly good as a side with red meat and game.

MACKEREL

Mackerel is one of the best fish that you can consume. I know it isn't always the most popular. However, it really is a supreme powerhouse of the omega 3 fatty acids so vital for the health of virtually every body system.

Omega 3 fatty acids have been shown to increase both the sensitivity and functionality of cell receptors, including insulin receptors. They also help to drastically reduce inflammation, something that diabetics face, particularly (and vitally) within the cardiovascular system. Mackerel is also a rich source of the mineral selenium, which can assist in reducing inflammation and also in enabling the body to manufacture its own antioxidant compounds.

OATS
Another of the better choices of grain for diabetics. They have a very low glycemic response, lots of fiber, and B vitamins. And they have another trick up their sleeve. One of the major risk factors for diabetics is cardiovascular disease. Oats have been proven to reduce cholesterol, by their soluble fiber binding to cholesterol in the digestive tract and carrying it away. A bowl of oatmeal a couple of times a week, or oaty toppings to vegetable crumbles, are great ways to get these in.

PARSNIPS
These are a great option as a stand-in for potatoes for Sunday lunches, or for a starchy side dish. This is for two reasons. Firstly, they have a very high fiber content, which will slow the release of the sugars present. Secondly, the majority of the sweet flavor that you detect when eating parsnips is given by something called inulin. This is a very complex sugar that, while small enough for our taste buds to detect, is actually complex enough to make it to the digestive tract intact, bypassing most of the absorption sites. Inulin has the added benefit of enhancing gut flora.

QUINOA
This is probably the champion of all of the grains and certainly my go-to grain of choice when I am eating a dish that would usually call for rice as an accompaniment. It has a super-low glycemic response and a very high protein content, creating the ultimate combination for even blood sugar in one single ingredient.

When you add other proteins and fat sources to it, you get a super slow-release meal. Quinoa also contains some essential fatty acids, magnesium, B vitamins, and even a small amount of iron.

SALMON
Another omega 3 powerhouse and one that definitely seems popular and palatable for most people. I would encourage you not to go for the ridiculously cheap cuts as they can have the lowest omega 3 levels. I'm not saying you need to splash out and buy wild Alaskan sockeye ... just a middle-of-the-road option. I prefer eating Scottish farmed salmon.

SQUASH
Squash is another great choice for a starchy carb source in place of potatoes. Again, it is high in fiber and also packed with carotenoids. Always leave the skin on to up the fiber content. Squash is slightly less versatile than potatoes, but will make a great mash and is just heavenly roasted as a side dish.

SWEET POTATOES
These are definitely one of my absolute favorite ingredients. As you have probably gathered by now, your regular everyday potato isn't the best food in the world for diabetics. Potatoes are like sugar bombs. However, sweet potatoes are a different animal. They have a much lower glycemic response, releasing their energy much more slowly. There is an added benefit in that they are rich in carotenoids that are beneficial for the skin and for the health of the cardiovascular system, a system that is at high risk in individuals with diabetes. Sweet potatoes have much of the versatility of regular potatoes and, in 99 percent of cases, can be used in place of them.

REFERENCES

Omega 3:

① Paquet C, Propsting SL. Total omega-3 fatty acid and SFA intakes in relation to insulin resistance in a Canadian First Nation at risk for the development of type 2 diabetes. 2013 Public Health Nutr, 21: 1–5

② Tsitouras PD1, Gucciardo F, Salbe AD, Heward C, Harman SM. 2008. High omega-3 fat intake improves insulin sensitivity and reduces CRP and IL6, but does not affect other endocrine axes in healthy older adults. Horm Metab Res. 40(3): 199–205

USEFUL CONTACTS & RESOURCES

Organizations

American Diabetes Association
The American Diabetes Association is the most widely known and prolific diabetes organisation in the US. Their website is a bit of a one-stop-shop for all the information you could need on treatment, self management, and support available.
diabetes.org

NUTRITIONAL RESOURCES

Academy of Nutrition and Dietetics
This website has lots of information on diabetes.
eatright.org

Nutritional supplements

Viridian Nutrition
Viridian nutrition make an extensive range of the cleanest supplements around. Over 180 products including vitamins, minerals, herbs, oils, and specific formulae made from the purest ingredients, with absolutely no additives, nasty fillers, or junk.
viridian-nutrition.com

RECIPES

Nutty oatmeal I'm not massively in favor of consuming too many grains when managing diabetes. However, some are certainly better than others and can form a small part of the diet. Oats are one of those. On their own I think they are still a little on the high GI side. But add some protein to the mix and it creates quite a slow-burner of a dish.

SERVES 1

½ cup (50 g) rolled oats
1½ cups (350 ml) milk of
    your choice (dairy or
    dairy-free)
½ tsp stevia
2 Tbsp crushed
    mixed nuts

Place the oats, milk, and stevia in a saucepan, set over low heat, and cook until the oats have softened and a creamy texture has formed.

Transfer to a bowl and top with the nuts. Add a small handful of berries as well, if desired, as an occasional treat.

Mixed vegetable frittata This is a lovely simple yet flavorsome breakfast.

SERVES 1
½ onion, minced
½ celery stalk,
   finely sliced
½ Tbsp olive oil
sea salt
1 large handful of
   baby spinach
2 large eggs,
   lightly beaten

Sauté the onion and celery in the olive oil in a small omelet pan, with a pinch of salt, until the onion softens. Meanwhile, preheat the broiler.

Add the spinach to the onion mixture and cook just until it wilts.

Pour the eggs over the vegetables and cook until you see the edges begin to set, but there is still uncooked egg in the center of the pan.

Place under the hot broiler until the remaining egg cooks through.

Spanish scramble

This is a lovely, tasty, bright dish that is super-quick to rustle up and can take the boredom factor out of breakfast time.

SERVES 1

¼ red onion, minced
½ red bell pepper, finely chopped
½ Tbsp olive oil
sea salt
6 cherry tomatoes, halved
2 eggs, lightly beaten
½ tsp mild smoked paprika
1 scallion, cut into julienne, to serve (optional)

Sauté the onion and pepper in the oil, with a pinch of salt, until the onion has softened and the pepper has begun to soften.

Add the tomatoes and sauté for another two or three minutes.

Add the eggs and paprika and continue stirring until the eggs have scrambled. Sprinkle with the scallion to serve, if desired.

Mixed greens and poached egg stack

It can take people a while to get their head around having vegetables, especially greens, at breakfast. But every meal is a chance to get nutrient-dense food into your diet and greens are common breakfasts in other parts of the world. Once you try it, I'm sure you will love it.

SERVES 1

handful of shredded
    collard greens
splash of white
    wine vinegar
1 large egg
handful of baby spinach
½ Tbsp olive oil
sea salt and freshly
    ground black pepper

Place the collard greens in a pan full of boiling water and blanch for a few minutes, until bright green and slightly softened. Drain and pat dry.

Bring a pan of water to a boil. Add a splash of vinegar to the water, crack in the egg, and poach for around four minutes.

Add the wilted greens and spinach to a separate pan, with the olive oil, salt, and pepper, and sauté just until the spinach has wilted.

Use a ring mold if you have one to compress the greens into a rounded stack. If not, you can compress them by hand. Top the greens with the poached egg to serve.

Smoked salmon, spinach, and dill omelet

This has a lovely Mediterranean or Nordic vibe to it. Spinach and dill are frequently combined in Greek cooking, while in Scandinavia, dill and salmon are a classic combination, paired in the dish gravadlax.

SERVES 1

2 large handfuls of spinach
½ Tbsp olive oil
2 eggs, lightly beaten
¼ oz (7 g) dill (just over one-quarter of a standard ¾-oz/20-g package)
2 slices of smoked salmon, torn into pieces

Sauté the spinach in the olive oil in a nonstick omelet pan until just wilted. Set aside.

Pour the eggs into the same pan and begin cooking the omelet until all the edges are done and the center is starting to turn.

Add the spinach to one half of the omelet, top with the dill and smoked salmon, then fold.

Kipper kedgeree I do love a good kedgeree. The traditional version is way too starchy, with its lashings of white rice. But swapping that for brown takes it down considerably.

SERVES 1
½ small red onion, minced
1 Tbsp olive oil
1 kippered herring fillet
½ tsp curry powder
⅓ cup (75 g) brown rice
handful of baby spinach
2 large eggs

Sauté the onion in the olive oil, until softened.

Cook the kippered herring according to the package directions. Many are boil in the bag. If the kippered herring is unpackaged from the store, broil or bake it for eight to 10 minutes.

Add the curry powder and rice to the onion, pour in enough water to cover, and simmer over high heat for around 20 minutes, until the rice is cooked. You may need to top off the water now and then during the cooking time. Meanwhile, hard-boil the eggs for about eight minutes, then shell them and cut into wedges.

Once the rice is nearly cooked, add the spinach and stir in until it wilts. Once the rice is cooked, flake in the kippered herring and mix well. Place the egg wedges on top.

Avocado, cilantro, and cheddar omelet, with spicy salsa

I first had this breakfast one early morning in LA, and fell in love with it. Now I have it at home and it brings a little bit of sunshine into my day!

SERVES 1

For the salsa
2 large tomatoes, finely chopped
¼ red onion, minced
leaves from a couple of sprigs of cilantro
hot sauce, to taste
sea salt and freshly ground black pepper

For the omelet
½ Tbsp olive oil
2 large eggs, lightly beaten
¼ avocado, finely chopped
handful of grated sharp cheddar

Combine all the salsa ingredients in a bowl, season, and mix well.

Pour the oil into an omelet pan and set it over medium-high heat. Add the eggs.

When the omelet is virtually cooked, add the avocado and cheddar. Continue cooking until the cheese has started to melt.

Transfer to a plate, folded if you want, then top with the salsa.

Low-carb eggs royale

This dish usually relies on sitting atop a toasted English muffin: full of starch! However, this version keeps the carbs at bay but still creates something for the eggs and salmon to sit on.

SERVES 1

2 large field mushrooms, stalks removed
splash of olive oil
2 eggs, plus 1 egg yolk
juice of ¼ lemon
⅓ cup (75 g) unsalted butter
splash of white wine vinegar
4 slices of smoked salmon

Gently fry the mushrooms in a small splash of olive oil, until they are fully cooked and nice and soft. Place these on a serving plate.

Bring a pan of water to a boil for the eggs, while you make the hollandaise.

Put the egg yolk and lemon juice into a blender or food processor. Melt the butter in a pan. When the butter is melted, switch the blender or processor onto low setting to begin breaking up the egg and lemon juice. Add 1 tsp of the melted butter and then another. As the mixture begins to emulsify, slowly pour in the remaining butter. Once it has all been added, turn up the speed of the machine to thicken the sauce.

Meanwhile, and working quickly, add a splash of vinegar to the water for the eggs, crack them in, and poach for around four minutes.

Place two smoked salmon slices on each mushroom. Top each one with a poached egg and pour over the hollandaise.

Chocolate cashew morning smoothie

This is the perfect option for those mornings when you need some breakfast but also need to fly out of the door. It can be made in seconds and is portable, too! Make sure you choose a low-carb whey protein powder that doesn't contain the hidden sugar that others can.

SERVES 1

scant 1 cup (200 ml) water or coconut water

1 heaping scoop of chocolate whey protein powder

1 tsp unsweetened cocoa

2 tsp cashew nut butter (available in health food stores)

Place all the ingredients into a blender and blend into a luxurious smoothie.

Lentil and bacon soup This old classic is perfect for keeping the blood sugar nice and even, not to mention the most important thing: it is a heavenly flavor combination.

SERVES 2

1 large red onion, minced
2 garlic cloves, minced
1 Tbsp olive oil
7 oz (200 g) smoked
  bacon pieces
¼ tsp turmeric
½ tsp ground coriander
scant 1½ cups (250 g) red
  lentils
generous 2 cups (500 ml)
  vegetable broth
sea salt and freshly
  ground black pepper
2 cherry tomatoes,
  chopped (optional)
4 sprigs of cilantro,
  chopped (optional)

Sauté the onion and garlic in the olive oil, until the onion starts to soften.

Add the bacon pieces and continue to sauté until they have cooked (about three or four minutes). Add the spices and mix well.

Stir in the lentils and one-third of the broth. Bring to a boil, then reduce the heat and let simmer until the broth reduces and the soup thickens, stirring frequently to avoid sticking. Add more broth little and often at this point, until the finished soup resembles a thin oatmeal. Season to taste and serve, with the chopped tomatoes and cilantro, if desired.

Quick chicken, arugula, and tahini wraps

This is a great option both for a quick lunch at home and as a portable meal to take to work or on a picnic. You can buy cooked chicken from the grocery store, for ultra convenience, though this is also a great way for using up leftover roast chicken.

SERVES 1

2¼ oz (65 g) cooked chicken breast, sliced
1 whole-wheat wrap
handful of arugula leaves
1 Tbsp tahini
juice of ½ lemon (optional)
sea salt and freshly ground black pepper

Place the chicken on top of the wrap, in a line across the center. Top with the arugula, then drizzle on the tahini.

Squeeze the lemon juice over and add a little salt and pepper, before wrapping.

Salad Niçoise with chicken

This classic salad needs little introduction. I just leave out the boiled potatoes to make it blood sugar-friendly and add chicken. This a great salad that is nutrient-dense but ideal for those days when you want something lighter, though its high protein content will still keep you full for ages!

SERVES 1

For the salad
1 chicken breast
1 egg
2 large handfuls of
   mixed salad greens
5 to 6 anchovy fillets
   (think of all that
   omega 3)
1 Tbsp black olives

For the dressing
1½ Tbsp olive oil
1 tsp balsamic vinegar
pinch of sea salt and
   freshly ground
   black pepper
¼ tsp dried mixed
   herbs, ideally herbes
   de Provence

Preheat the oven to 400°F/200°C.

Bake the chicken breast for 15 to 20 minutes. Let cool slightly, then slice.

Meanwhile, boil the egg for about eight minutes, then drain, peel, and slice.

Combine the salad greens, anchovies, boiled egg, and olives and mix well.

Combine the dressing ingredients and whisk to emulsify. Use it to dress the salad and toss well.

Place the sliced chicken breast on top.

Fava bean, mint, and feta salad I love this combination of flavors. Beautifully complementary and a low-GI treat.

SERVES 1

3½ cups (400 g) fava
   beans
7 to 8 mint leaves
1 Tbsp pitted black
   olives, chopped
juice of ½ lemon
handful of arugula
   leaves (optional)
2½ oz (70 g) feta cheese
sea salt and freshly
   ground black pepper

Bring a saucepan of water to a boil, add the beans, and boil for three minutes. Tip into a colander and let cool. If your beans are a little on the mature side, pinch each one in your fingers; the skins should slip off to reveal a bright green bean underneath.

Mix the drained beans with the mint leaves, olives, and lemon juice, with the arugula, if desired, tossing well.

Top with the crumbled feta cheese and season to taste.

Egg and watercress rye open sandwich
Quick, tasty, and nutrient-dense.

SERVES 1
2 hard-boiled eggs
1 Tbsp mayonnaise
sea salt and freshly
    ground black pepper
1 slice of pumpernickel
    bread
handful of watercress

Mash the hard-boiled eggs with the mayonnaise and a little salt and pepper.

Spread the egg mixture on the pumpernickel bread, then top with the watercress.

Mackerel mayo avocado boats This is an upmarket, nutritionally boosted version of those old-school shrimp cocktails that would often come served in half an avocado. Good fats ahoy on this one! Use ready-cooked mackerel fillets from the grocery store.

SERVES 1
2 cooked mackerel fillets
1 Tbsp mayonnaise
juice of ½ lemon
sea salt and freshly
   ground black pepper
1 very ripe avocado

Remove the skin from the mackerel fillets and break the fillets into a bowl in small pieces. Add the mayonnaise, lemon juice, sea salt, and black pepper and mix well.

Halve the avocado and remove the pit.

Place the mackerel mixture into the indentations in the avocado and out over the flesh. Serve with a good side salad.

Feta, tomato, and black olive stuffed peppers

These have a beautiful Mediterranean vibe going on. In the summer they are great with a side salad, while in the winter they go perfectly with a bit of sweet potato mash (see page 114) and some cooked greens.

SERVES 1

1 large red bell pepper, halved and seeded
½ red onion, minced
½ Tbsp olive oil
5 cherry tomatoes, chopped
sea salt and freshly ground black pepper
10 pitted kalamata olives, chopped (other black olives will be fine)
7 oz (200 g) feta cheese

Preheat the oven to 400°F/200°C.

Place the pepper halves cut side down on a baking sheet. Add a small amount of water to the tray and place at the top of the hot oven for 10 to 12 minutes, until the pepper is starting to soften and the skin is beginning to wrinkle.

Meanwhile, in a pan, sauté the red onion in the oil until it has softened. Add the tomatoes and a pinch of salt and pepper and continue cooking until a thick tomato sauce has formed. Add the olives and stir well.

Remove the peppers from the oven, discarding excess water if there is any left in the baking tray. Turn the peppers over so they can be filled. Stuff with the tomato mixture and crumble over the feta cheese. Return to the oven for another 10 minutes.

Serve with a good side salad, or cooked vegetables of your choice.

Minted beet houmous and goat cheese salad bowl

This slightly crazy creation was another of those happy accidents that arose from needing to use up some leftovers. What came out was a splendidly flavorsome and filling dish. Very nutrient-dense, this will keep you going for ages.

SERVES 1

2 cooked beets
1½ cups (200 g) canned chickpeas, drained
4 to 5 mint leaves, chopped
1 small garlic clove, minced
½ Tbsp olive oil
sea salt
2¼ oz (60 g) goat cheese
2 handfuls of mixed salad greens

Place the beets, chickpeas, mint, garlic, olive oil, and a pinch of sea salt in a blender or food processor and process into a thick houmous.

Place a generous dollop of this houmous into the center of a large salad bowl.

Crumble the goat cheese on top and then surround with the salad greens.

Stir-fried shrimp and zucchini ribbons with cashews and goji berries This is a speedy but very tasty lunch. Hot lunches can be a bit of a rigmarole. Not this one!

SERVES 1

1 large zucchini
2 garlic cloves, minced
½ small red chile, minced
2 scallions, sliced lengthwise
1 Tbsp olive oil
sea salt
3½ oz (100 g) raw king shrimp, shelled and deveined if necessary
2 tsp soy sauce
1 tsp sesame oil
10 cashews
1 Tbsp goji berries

Trim off both ends of the zucchini and then, using a vegetable peeler, cut the zucchini into long ribbons.

Stir-fry the zucchini ribbons, garlic, chile, and scallions in the olive oil with a pinch of sea salt for around two minutes.

Add the king shrimp and carry on stir-frying until the shrimp have cooked. Add the soy sauce and sesame oil and combine well.

Sprinkle over the cashews and goji berries to serve.

Curried tuna salad with citrus omega dressing

This is such a wonderful salad. Everyone thinks of salad as a summer staple only, but the nutrients you get from raw vegetables and fruits are vital to support your health through the winter, too. So don't be afraid of going for a salad at any time of the year. This one always works a treat.

SERVES 1

For the salad
1 cup minus 1 Tbsp (120 g) canned tuna, drained
1 Tbsp mayonnaise
½ tsp mild curry powder
1 scallion, minced
handful of mixed baby leaf salad
½ red bell pepper, finely chopped

For the dressing
juice of ½ lime
small bunch of cilantro, coarsely chopped
1 Tbsp flaxseed oil
1 tsp agave nectar
sea salt and freshly ground black pepper

Mix the tuna, mayonnaise, curry powder, and scallion together.

Place the tuna on a plate and surround with the salad greens and red pepper.

Combine all the dressing ingredients and mix well to ensure they are emulsified. Use it to dress the salad greens and tuna.

Spinach baked eggs
This lunch is insanely easy and seriously tasty and satisfying. It's perfect for a lazy day at the weekend.

SERVES 1

1 garlic clove, minced
1 Tbsp olive oil
sea salt
4 cups (200 g) baby spinach (this sounds a lot but it wilts to nothing)
2 large eggs
2¼ oz (60 g) feta cheese

Preheat the oven to 400°F/200°C.

Sauté the garlic in the olive oil with a pinch of salt for one or two minutes, to the point it is starting to get fragrant.

Add the baby spinach, one handful at a time, stirring well. You will find it wilts down very quickly. As it does so, add the next handful and so on, until it is all cooked.

Transfer the spinach to a small individual ovenproof dish. Make two wells in the spinach, and crack an egg into each well.

Place the dish in the oven and bake for about eight minutes. You will find the eggs almost cooked, with some of the whites still not quite there. At this stage, crumble over the feta cheese, then return to the oven for a final four or five minutes, for the egg whites to cook fully.

Cheeky chopped salad

I love a good chopped salad. They are very popular, so I'm sure once you try my version of a chopped salad you will love it as much as I do.

SERVES 1

For the salad
2 large handfuls of
    mixed salad greens
½ avocado, peeled
    and chopped
1 cooked chicken
    breast, chopped
½ cup (60 g) crumbled
    Danish blue cheese

For the dressing
½ Tbsp olive oil
½ Tbsp mayonnaise
½ tsp cider vinegar
½ tsp garlic granules
pinch of sea salt

Place the salad greens in a serving bowl and top with the avocado, chicken, and blue cheese.

Combine all the dressing ingredients and mix well to emulsify. Top the salad with the dressing.

Griddled halloumi with roasted vegetables and seeded quinoa

This simple yet satisfying dinner is certainly a favorite of mine during the warmer months, but brings a bit of sunshine into colder days, too.

SERVES 1 TO 2

½ small zucchini, cut into circles
½ red bell pepper, finely chopped
1 large red onion, halved and sliced
1½ Tbsp olive oil
sea salt and freshly ground black pepper
½ tsp mild smoked paprika
½ tsp garlic granules
scant ½ cup (75 g) quinoa
3 Tbsp mixed seeds
4 slices halloumi cheese (3½ to 4¼ oz/ 100 to 120 g in total)

Preheat the oven to 400°F/200°C.

Place the chopped vegetables in a roasting pan. Drizzle with 1 Tbsp of the olive oil and season with a pinch of sea salt, black pepper, the paprika, and garlic granules. Mix well to ensure the vegetables are evenly covered, then roast at the top of the hot oven for around 20 minutes, stirring regularly.

Place the quinoa into a pan and cover with just-boiled water. Simmer for around 20 minutes, until small tail-like shoots develop on the side of the grain and it is soft to the bite. Drain, stir in the seeds and a little sea salt, and set aside.

In a ridged grill pan (or a small skillet), heat the remaining ½ Tbsp of olive oil and griddle or fry the halloumi until it turns golden brown on each side. Serve the quinoa with the roast veg and halloumi on top.

Speedy chicken and lentil curry This dish is one-pot wonder cooking at its very best. A ready-made curry paste makes it an ideal option for when you want something virtuous, but don't want to spend forever in the kitchen.

SERVES 1 TO 2
1 red onion, minced
2 garlic cloves, minced
1 Tbsp olive or
    coconut oil
sea salt
1 Tbsp your favorite
    curry paste
⅔ cup (125 g) red lentils
generous 2 cups (500 ml)
    vegetable broth (you
    may not need it all)
1 large chicken
    breast, chopped
handful of cilantro,
    to serve (optional)
lime wedges, to serve
    (optional)

Sauté the onion and garlic in the olive or coconut oil, with a pinch of salt, until the onion has softened. Add the curry paste and stir for around a minute, until the spices in the paste are becoming more aromatic.

Add the lentils and a little of the vegetable broth. Keep adding the broth little and often, in a similar way to cooking a risotto. When you notice the liquid reducing, add a little more, and so on.

Once the lentils are cooked (soft and starting to fall apart), add the chicken and keep simmering away until the chicken is cooked: cut open one of the largest pieces; it should be opaque and white to the center with no trace of pink. If it's not quite ready, cook for a minute or two more, then check again.

Serve sprinkled with cilantro, with lime wedges on the side, if desired.

Tofu soba stir-fry This quick noodle stir-fry is really flavorsome and contains quite the array of nutrients. Soba noodles are made from buckwheat, which contains some powerful antioxidant compounds, such as rutin. They come premeasured into portion-size bundles in the packages.

SERVES 1
1 bundle of soba noodles
1 large red onion, halved, then sliced widthwise
2 garlic cloves, minced
1 Tbsp olive oil
sea salt
3 to 4 mushrooms, sliced
3½ oz (100 g) marinated tofu, chopped into cubes
3 tsp tamari soy sauce
1 tsp toasted sesame oil
a few sprigs of cilantro, chopped

Place the soba noodles in a pan full of boiling water and cook for around eight minutes.

Meanwhile, in a wok or large skillet, stir-fry the onion and garlic in the olive oil and a pinch of sea salt, until the onion has softened. Add the mushrooms and tofu and continue to stir-fry until the mushrooms are cooked.

Drain the noodles, then add these to the pan and mix well to make sure the vegetables and tofu are well mixed through.

Add the tamari and sesame oil and mix well. Sprinkle over the cilantro and serve.

King shrimp and greens in satay sauce

This is a sure-fire winner. So simple, but oozing with exotic flavor and so nutrient-dense that it will seriously fill you up. Ticks every box, I reckon.

SERVES 1 TO 2

1 large red onion, minced
2 garlic cloves, minced
½ Tbsp olive oil
sea salt
2 large handfuls of shredded greens of your choice: kale or collard greens work best
3½ oz (100 g) cooked king shrimp, shelled and deveined if necessary
2 tsp soy sauce
1 tsp honey
1 heaping Tbsp peanut butter
½ tsp five spice
small bunch of cilantro, coarsely chopped

Sauté the onion and garlic in the olive oil, with a pinch of sea salt, until the onion softens.

Add the greens and the shrimp and continue to sauté for another three to five minutes, until the greens have started to wilt and are turning a deeper green color.

Add the soy sauce, honey, peanut butter, and five spice and mix well.

Add the chopped cilantro before serving.

Pesto-roast salmon with buttered greens

This really is as simple as it gets but there is such richness of flavor and a huge amount of nutrition, the all-important omega 3 fatty acids being the stars of the show! Don't be scared off by the butter, I'd rather use that than artificial margarine any day ... just don't go nuts!

SERVES 1
1 large salmon fillet
2 Tbsp basil pesto
4⅔ cup cups (280 g) mixed green vegetables (peas, chopped leeks, and shredded cabbage are a great combo)
2 tsp unsalted butter
sea salt and freshly ground black pepper

Preheat the oven to 400°F/200°C.

Place the salmon on a baking sheet and bake at the top of the hot oven for 10 to 12 minutes. Remove, top with the pesto, and return to the oven for another 10 to 12 minutes, or until the edges of the pesto begin to get a little crispy.

Place the mixed greens into a pan with the butter and sauté for up to 10 minutes (don't cook them to death). Season well.

Serve the greens mounded up on the plate with the salmon on top.

Mediterranean sweet potato and chickpea stew

This is real comfort food, but also has the type of flavor that is satisfying at any time of the year. This is what I call clean food and it's also super-filling and really easy.

SERVES 2

1 large red onion, minced
2 garlic cloves, minced
1 Tbsp olive oil
sea salt
½ large sweet potato, chopped, skin-on
1½ cups (400 g) canned chickpeas, drained
2 cups (400 g) canned chopped tomatoes
1¼ cups (300 ml) vegetable broth (you may not need it all)
2 Tbsp pitted black olives, coarsely chopped

Sauté the onion and garlic in the olive oil, with a pinch of sea salt, until the onion has softened.

Add the sweet potato, chickpeas, and tomatoes, bring to a boil, then reduce the heat and simmer for around 20 minutes, until the sweet potato is soft. You may notice that during this cooking time the liquid reduces significantly. This is where the vegetable broth comes in. Add it in small amounts to moisten when needed.

Taste, then season further. Add the olives and mix well.

White beans with spinach, roasted fennel, and garlic I find this amazing comfort food! The creamy texture is really pleasing.

SERVES 1 TO 2
1 fennel bulb, sliced
1 Tbsp olive oil
sea salt and freshly
 ground black pepper
2 garlic cloves, minced
2 cups (400 g) canned
 cannellini beans, half
 drained
2 handfuls of baby
 spinach

Preheat the oven to 400°F/200°C.

Place the fennel in a baking sheet and drizzle with half the olive oil, salt, and pepper. Place at the top of the hot oven and roast for 15 to 20 minutes.

Meanwhile, in a pan, sauté the garlic in the remaining olive oil with a pinch of sea salt. Cook it on high heat, as this is one occasion where you want the garlic to catch and brown. This delivers a lovely smoky flavor.

Add the half-drained beans and the spinach and cook for five minutes, until the spinach wilts.

Place the bean mixture on a plate and top with the roasted fennel.

Baked sweet potato with mixed beans, zucchini, and pesto This is the ultimate in simple suppers and great for those days when you want something filling, but don't want to faff around in the kitchen forever.

SERVES 1

1 medium sweet potato
½ zucchini, sliced
    into circles
½ Tbsp olive oil
sea salt
2 cups (400 g) canned
    mixed beans, drained
2 Tbsp basil pesto

Preheat the oven to 425°F/220°C.

Prick the sweet potato all over with a knife and bake at the top of the hot oven for about one hour. The potato should be soft throughout.

Sauté the zucchini in the olive oil, along with a pinch of sea salt, until it softens. Add the beans and pesto and mix well.

Top the baked sweet potato with the pesto beans. Scoff.

Goat cheese and roasted butternut squash salad

A salad may sound a bit light for dinner, but there is so much substance to this one that it really does keep you going. Plus it tastes amazing, too. Got to be a winner!

SERVES 1

For the salad
¼ small butternut
   squash, sliced quite
   chunky, skin-on
½ Tbsp olive oil
sea salt and freshly
   ground black pepper
handful of arugula leaves
handful of baby spinach
5 cherry tomatoes, halved
⅓ cup (75 g) soft goat
   cheese
1 Tbsp walnuts
1 Tbsp mixed seeds

For the dressing
1 Tbsp extra virgin
   olive oil
1 tsp balsamic vinegar
½ tsp dried mixed herbs

Preheat the oven to 400°F/200°C.

Place the butternut squash in a roasting pan and drizzle with the olive oil, salt, and pepper. Place at the top of the hot oven and roast for about 20 minutes, turning occasionally, until soft and turning golden brown.

Mix together the dressing ingredients and whisk to create an emulsion.

Assemble the salad by mixing the leaves and tomatoes together. Top with the roasted squash, crumble on the goat cheese, pour over the dressing, and finish with the walnuts and seeds.

Mediterranean chicken meatloaf

This is seriously hearty fare. Great on a cold winter's evening with some roasted root vegetables and steamed greens, but equally at home on a blazing summer's day with a salad.

SERVES 2 TO 4

2¼ cups (500 g) ground chicken
1 large egg, lightly beaten
2 garlic cloves, minced
8 to 10 sundried tomatoes, coarsely chopped
½ tsp dried oregano
sea salt and freshly ground black pepper
olive oil, for the pan

Preheat the oven to 400°F/200°C.

Mix all the ingredients together in a large bowl. Season, then press the mix into an oiled loaf pan.

Bake for 35 minutes. Remove from the oven and let cool slightly before slicing. Serve with roasted veg, or salad. You can even use cold leftover slices in sandwiches and wraps.

Miso mackerel with bok choy

This is another speedy dinner. I first tried mackerel with miso when I was in Japan and I became hooked: two intense flavors colliding. Miso is available everywhere now, any grocery store will have it.

SERVES 2

2 mackerel fillets
7 oz (200 g) bok choy
1 garlic clove, minced
½ Tbsp olive oil
sea salt
2 Tbsp miso paste

Preheat the oven to 400°F/200°C.

Place the mackerel on a baking sheet and bake for about 20 minutes. I love it when the edges begin to get a little crispy, so there are a few more textures going on.

Separate the bok choy leaves from their stem. Stir-fry the bok choy with the garlic in the oil, with a good pinch of sea salt.

Place the miso paste into a small pitcher, add about 1 Tbsp of boiling water, and mix together to make a thinner, pourable paste.

Plate the greens and mackerel up and pour the miso paste over the fish.

Peppered cod with fennel barlotto and baby leaf salad This is really a fancy little dish but is actually very easy to make. It's a great dinner party main course.

SERVES 2

1 large onion, minced
2 garlic cloves, minced
1 large fennel bulb,
    finely chopped
3 Tbsp olive oil, plus more
    for the baking sheet
sea salt and cracked
    black pepper
1⅓ cups (250 g) pearl
    barley
4½ cups (1 liter)
    vegetable broth
2 cod fillets
2 tsp balsamic vinegar
2 handfuls of mixed
    baby salad greens
handful of parsley
    leaves (optional)

Begin by sautéing the onion, garlic, and fennel in 1 Tbsp of the olive oil and a good pinch of sea salt, until the vegetables start to soften.

Add the pearl barley, mix well, then add a small amount of broth. Keep stirring in broth every few minutes as it reduces, little and often, until the dish resembles risotto. Pearl barley does take considerably longer to cook than rice would—maybe up to 40 minutes—but really is worth it. Meanwhile, preheat the oven to 400°F/200°C.

Place the cod on a lightly oiled baking sheet and sprinkle with cracked black pepper. Bake at the top of the hot oven for 15 to 20 minutes.

Mix the remaining 2 Tbsp of olive oil and the balsamic vinegar together and whisk well to emulsify. Use this to dress the baby greens.

Place a good serving of the barlotto in the center of two serving plates, then top with the fish, the parsley (if using), and a handful of the greens.

Lemongrass chicken stew

This is a beautiful fusion-style dish that is halfway between a hearty stew and a Thai curry. It is a sure-fire family favorite in the making! Give the fresh lemongrass a good bashing with a rolling pin (thinking of your boss might help). This releases the oils, for greater flavor.

SERVES 2

1 large red onion, minced
3 garlic cloves, minced
2 stalks of lemongrass, bashed
1 Tbsp olive oil
sea salt
1⅓ cups (250 g) red lentils
1¾ cups (400 g) canned coconut milk
up to 1¾ cups (400 ml) vegetable broth
3 medium chicken breasts, cut into bite-size pieces

Sauté the onion, garlic, and lemongrass in the olive oil, with a good pinch of salt, until the onion softens.

Add the lentils and the coconut milk and let simmer for about five minutes. The liquid will reduce in volume very quickly. Start adding a small amount of broth. Treat this dish a bit like a risotto from now on, adding small amounts of broth bit by bit as the lentils soften. That's why I say up to 1¾ cups (400 ml) of vegetable broth. You might not need it all, it's just there for back up!

When the lentils are starting to soften and are partially breaking down, add the chicken. Continue cooking as above until the chicken is cooked: cut open one of the largest pieces; it should be opaque and white in the center with no trace of pink. If it's not quite ready, cook for a minute or two more, then check again. Serve with a salad.

Salmon and shrimp burgers with cilantro cashew quinoa This is a great recipe for the summer months, as it is bursting with exotic flavors. It can work just as well in a bun with salad for a satisfying lunch.

SERVES 2

9¼ oz (260 g) cooked shrimp, deveined if necessary
2 skinless salmon fillets, chopped
2 garlic cloves, minced
2 Tbsp green curry paste
2 eggs, lightly beaten
sea salt and cracked black pepper
ground flaxseed, if needed (available in health food stores)
generous 1 cup (200 g) quinoa
5 Tbsp cashews
leaves from a small bunch of cilantro, coarsely chopped
½ Tbsp olive oil

Place the shrimp, salmon, garlic, curry paste, eggs, and a pinch of sea salt into a food processor and process to a smooth ground texture. If it is a little too wet (natural variation in produce can sometimes vary), use ground flaxseed to stiffen the mix up to a texture that is workable by hand.

Remove the mixture, divide into four, and form into burger patty shapes.

Meanwhile, place the quinoa in a saucepan, cover with boiling water, and let simmer for 20 minutes, or until softened.

Drain the quinoa and stir in the cashews, chopped cilantro, sea salt, and cracked black pepper. Set aside.

Fry the salmon burgers in the oil for about five minutes on each side.

Serve the burgers over the quinoa.

Omega herb-crusted salmon with spiced sweet potato mash and wilted greens

This is a deeply flavorsome dish that feels really hearty and homely. Definitely a feel-good dish for the colder evenings!

SERVES 2

4 Tbsp ground flaxseed (available in health food stores)
2 Tbsp whole-wheat bread crumbs
2 tsp dried basil
2 tsp dried oregano
2 tsp dried rosemary
1 garlic clove, crushed
2 Tbsp olive oil
2 large salmon fillets
1 large sweet potato, chopped
4 handfuls of sliced greens (collard greens or chard work best)
small piece of unsalted butter
½ tsp pumpkin pie spice
sea salt

Preheat the oven to 400°F/200°C.

Mix the ground flax, bread crumbs, herbs, garlic, and olive oil to make the topping.

Spread the mixture over the salmon fillets and place on a foil-lined baking sheet.

Place in the oven for 15 to 20 minutes, until the crust has become golden brown.

Meanwhile, place the sweet potato in a pan and cover with water. Bring to a boil, then reduce the heat and simmer for 10 to 15 minutes, until soft. (An even better option, if possible, is to steam it to retain the nutrients.)

Steam or blanch the greens in hot water for three or four minutes, just until wilted.

Drain the water from the sweet potato and mash. Add the butter, pumpkin pie spice, and a pinch of salt and mash again until smooth and all the ingredients are thoroughly mixed.

Serve with the salmon and greens.

Tilapia with pea, mint, and feta mash and balsamic tomato salad This is such a colorful, light, and vibrant dish; big on flavor and big on nutrients.

SERVES 2

2⅔ cups (300 g) peas
   (frozen are fine here)
sea salt and freshly
   ground black pepper
2 tilapia fillets
1½ Tbsp olive oil
1 tsp balsamic vinegar
scant 1 cup (150 g) cherry
   tomatoes, halved
3 oz (80 g) feta cheese

Place the peas in a pan and cover with boiling water. Simmer for about 15 minutes, until nice and soft. Strain, then mash using a potato masher, or place in a food processor and pulse on low setting to make a mash. Season well and set aside.

Fry the seasoned tilapia in ½ Tbsp of the olive oil for about 12 minutes, turning frequently, until golden brown.

Mix the remaining 1 Tbsp of olive oil and the balsamic vinegar together, whisking to emulsify. Use it to dress the tomatoes.

Very gently reheat the pea mash, crumbling in the feta cheese

Plate up the mash. Top with the tilapia fillet and serve with the tomato salad.

Thai green vegetable curry with brown basmati rice

A Thai green curry, made from scratch, tastes like heaven. This is a bit more time-consuming and may seem a little unnerving at first. But, give it a go, you'll see how simple it is and how incredible it tastes!

SERVES 2

For the curry paste
2 lemongrass stalks, minced
2 green chiles
2 garlic cloves
1 large onion, chopped
½-in (1-cm) piece of gingerroot, chopped
1½ cups (30 g) cilantro
4 basil leaves
4 kaffir lime leaves
½ tsp white pepper
½ tsp ground coriander
3 Tbsp Thai fish sauce
1 tsp shrimp paste
juice of 1 lime

For the curry
1 Tbsp virgin coconut oil
1 large zucchini, sliced
½ red bell pepper, chopped
¼ eggplant, chopped
6 to 7 baby corn
1½ cups (100 g) sliced shiitake mushrooms
2 handfuls baby spinach
1¾ cups (400 g) coconut milk
1 cup (200 ml) vegetable broth
1 cup (180 g) brown rice

Place all the paste ingredients in a food processor and blend into a pungent aromatic paste. (A word of warning from bitter experience: don't inhale deeply when you take the lid off the processor. You have been warned.)

Fry the paste in the virgin coconut oil, until it turns a darker, duller green and is less pungent in aroma.

Add the vegetables, coconut milk, and vegetable broth, bring to a boil, then reduce the heat and simmer until the vegetables have cooked.

Meanwhile, simmer the rice according to the package directions, until cooked and fluffy. Serve the curry with the rice on the side.

Sea bass with roasted fennel and spiced root vegetable mash Simple, deeply flavored, and as easy as it gets!

SERVES 2

1 large fennel bulb
1½ Tbsp olive oil
sea salt and freshly
　ground black pepper
1 medium sweet potato,
　skin-on, chopped
2 medium parsnips,
　skins-on, chopped
½ tsp pumpkin pie spice
2 sea bass fillets

Preheat the oven to 400°F/200°C.

Slice the fennel bulb into long thin slices and place on a baking sheet. Drizzle with 1 Tbsp of the olive oil and add a pinch of sea salt. Mix well, then roast at the top of the hot oven for about 20 minutes, turning occasionally.

Place the sweet potato and parsnips in a pan and cover with boiling water. Simmer for around 20 minutes, until softened. Mash with a potato masher—or place in a food processor and pulse on low setting—to form a mash. Remember, with the skins left on the veg, a more rustic texture will be given. If you don't like this, feel free to peel them instead. Stir in the spice and season to taste.

Gently fry the sea bass fillet in the remaining ½ Tbsp of oil for about 10 minutes, turning frequently, until golden brown.

Serve the fish on the mash with steamed greens.

Glazed salmon with spiced vegetables and coconut rice

Adding coconut to the rice here is a great way of adding interest to the texture and flavor of an everyday side dish, plus it really complements the spicing.

SERVES 2

1 Tbsp runny honey
1½ tsp Dijon mustard
2 large salmon steaks
4 handfuls of brown rice
1¾ cups (400 ml) canned
   coconut milk
2 Tbsp dry unsweetened
   coconut
1 garlic clove
1 large red onion,
   halved and sliced
1 small zucchini,
   cut into circles
1 red bell pepper, sliced
scant 2¼ cups (150 g)
   sliced shiitake
   mushrooms
1 Tbsp olive oil
handful of baby spinach
¼ tsp garam masala
¼ tsp ground cumin
¼ tsp ground cinnamon

Mix together the honey and mustard. Marinate the salmon in this mixture in a bowl for as long as possible (overnight is best, one hour will do).

Place the rice in a pan with the coconut milk and simmer until the coconut milk notably reduces, stirring frequently to avoid sticking. Add water (up to about 2 cups/500 ml) in small increments until the rice has cooked and a thick rice pudding texture has been reached. Stir in the dry unsweetened coconut.

Add the garlic, onion, and vegetables to a pan and sauté in the oil until the vegetables soften. Then add the spinach and the spices and sauté for another minute.

Add the salmon and its marinade to a separate pan set over medium heat and cook for 10 to 12 minutes, turning every couple of minutes to avoid blackening.

Serve the salmon on the coconut rice with the vegetables on the side.

Seafood fried rice with garlic greens

This little dish is really just wholesome home food at its best. It isn't overly complicated but it's a perfect dish to have in the middle of the table that everyone can just dive into. It's a bit like a more virtuous paella vibe.

SERVES 2

¾ cup (150 g) brown basmati rice
2 garlic cloves, minced
1 large red onion, minced
1½ Tbsp olive oil
sea salt and freshly ground black pepper
7 oz (200 g) precooked mixed seafood
1 Tbsp soy sauce
2 tsp sesame oil
½ tsp mild curry powder
4 handfuls of shredded greens
1 scallion, cut into julienne, to serve (optional)

Place the rice in a saucepan and cook according to the package directions until soft. Drain and set aside.

Sauté half the garlic and all the red onion in 1 Tbsp of the olive oil, with a pinch of sea salt, until the onion has softened. Add the seafood and sauté for another one or two minutes.

Stir in the rice. Add the soy sauce, sesame oil, and curry powder and mix well.

Sauté the greens in the remaining ½ Tbsp of olive oil for two or three minutes, just until they are beginning to wilt. Add the remaining garlic, mix well, and season to taste.

Serve the rice with the greens on the side, sprinkled with scallion (if using).

Bacon-wrapped chicken breast with herbed spinach puy lentils This is hearty wholesome home-cooked food at its best.

SERVES 2
1 large red onion, minced
½ Tbsp olive oil
sea salt
1¾ cups (300 g) Puy lentils
generous 2 cups (500 ml) vegetable broth
3 handfuls of baby spinach
leaves from a large bunch of parsley, coarsely chopped
2 large skinless boneless chicken breasts
4 slices of smoked bacon

Preheat the oven to 400°F/200°C.

Sauté the onion in the olive oil with a pinch of sea salt, until softened.

Add the Puy lentils and a small amount of broth. Simmer until the broth begins to reduce. Keep adding the broth little and often until the lentils are cooked. At the last minute, add the spinach and cook just until it wilts. Add the chopped parsley and mix well.

Meanwhile, wrap each chicken breast securely with 2 slices of bacon. Place them on a baking sheet and bake at the top of the oven for around 25 minutes.

Place a serving of lentils in the middle of two plates and top each with a chicken breast.

Tandoori chicken with garden pea dal This is a great winter dish. It is perfect for those days when you want warming, wholesome comfort food. Big on flavor, big on feel-good factor!

SERVES 2

generous 1 cup (280 ml) plain yogurt
2 tsp ground cumin, plus ½ tsp for the dal
½ tsp turmeric, plus ½ tsp for the dal
2 tsp garam masala
½ tsp ground coriander
½ tsp chili powder
juice of ½ lemon
6 garlic cloves, minced
sea salt
2 large chicken breasts
1 Tbsp olive or coconut oil
1 cup (200 g) red lentils
generous 2 cups (500 ml) vegetable broth (you may not need it all)
1 cup (100 g) peas (frozen are fine here)
handful of cilantro leaves, to serve (optional)

Make the tandoori marinade by mixing the yogurt, spices, lemon juice, and four of the garlic cloves along with a pinch of sea salt. Mix well to make a spicy paste.

Place the chicken into a deep dish. Score the flesh, pour the marinade over the top, cover, and marinate in the refrigerator for three or four hours.

When ready to cook, preheat the oven to 400°F/200°C. Place the chicken breasts on a baking sheet and bake at the top of the oven for around 20 minutes.

Meanwhile, sauté the remaining garlic in the olive or coconut oil and let the garlic catch and brown to give a smoky flavor. Add the lentils and cover with a small amount of broth, adding it little and often, as much as needed, until the lentils are beginning to break down. Remove one-third of the mixture, place in a blender, and blend to a smooth puree. Return it to the remaining mixture. Add the peas, cumin, and turmeric and cook until the peas soften.

Chop the chicken and serve on top of the dal, sprinkled with cilantro leaves, if desired.

Cod with leek puree and baby green salad

This is a great dish as it is speedy, looks a bit "restauranty" and tastes lovely. A nice one to pull out at dinner parties.

SERVES 2

2 cod fillets
sea salt and freshly
    ground black pepper
4 large leeks, sliced
    into rings
3 garlic cloves, minced
½ Tbsp olive oil
3 handfuls of baby
    salad greens

For the dressing
1 Tbsp olive oil
1 tsp balsamic vinegar

Preheat the oven to 400°F/200°C.

Place the cod fillets on a baking sheet and season with a little salt and pepper. Bake in the oven for about 15 minutes.

Sauté the leeks and garlic in the oil with a pinch of sea salt, for five to eight minutes, until the leeks are nice and soft. Transfer to a blender or food processor, add 1 Tbsp of water, then blend into a puree.

Mix the salad dressing ingredients and whisk to emulsify. Dress the salad greens and toss well.

Place a generous helping of the puree on the serving plates and spread out with the back of a spoon. Place the cod fillets on top of the puree. Top each cod fillet with a good handful of the dressed baby salad.

Cheeky chocolate pots These are my old faithful healthy choccie dessert of choice. The ingredients may sound an odd combination but—seriously—give them a bash. I'm pretty sure you will be pleasantly surprised.

SERVES 2 TO 3

2 large, very ripe avocados, peeled and pitted
2 to 3 Tbsp unsweetened cocoa, to taste
1 Tbsp melted coconut oil
up to 1 tsp stevia, to taste

Place all the ingredients in a food processor and blend to a smooth chocolatey dessert.

Place in ramekins or serving glasses, then refrigerate for one hour before serving.

Vanilla frozen yogurt This high-protein dessert is sweet, creamy, and satisfying.

SERVES 3

scant 3 cups (675 g) natural live probiotic yogurt

1½ cups (150 g) vanilla protein powder

1 tsp vanilla extract

3 tsp coconut oil, melted

Blend all the ingredients well.

If you have an ice-cream maker, transfer the mixture to that and freeze according to the manufacturer's guidelines.

If not, pour the mixture into a freezerproof container and transfer to the freezer. After about 30 minutes, check the mix. If ice crystals are forming, remove and stir the mix well. Return to the freezer, then repeat the stirring process after 30 minutes more. Keep doing this until a frozen yogurt/ice cream texture is reached.

Low-GI cheesecake

I love a good cheesecake, but the amount of sugar you find in most is horrific. This version is incredibly low GI. With an almost savory base and a filling that is sweetened with stevia, it is a dessert that ticks all the right boxes!

SERVES 4

For the base
½ cup plus 2 Tbsp (75 g) mixed nuts
2¼ oz (65 g) rough oatcakes
1½ Tbsp melted coconut oil

For the filling
1½ cups (350 g) cream cheese
1½ cups (350 g) mascarpone cheese
2 tsp stevia
3 Tbsp coconut oil, melted
2 tsp vanilla extract
2 cartons of blueberries

Place the nuts and oatcakes in a food processor and grind to a coarse texture. Add the coconut oil and process again until well mixed.

Press the mixture into a 9-in (23-cm) springform pan and place in the freezer, while you work on making the filling.

Mix the cream cheese, mascarpone, stevia, melted coconut oil, and vanilla extract together in a bowl and mix well.

Remove the springform pan from the freezer, cover the base with the filling, and smooth the surface. Top with the blueberries and refrigerate for three to five hours.

Three-seed spread This is like a funky peanut butter-houmous hybrid. Better still, it is packed with fatty acids and protein!

MAKES 8 TO 10 PORTIONS

½ cup (75 g) hulled (shelled) hemp seeds
½ cup (75 g) pumpkin seeds
½ cup (75 g) flaxseeds
1 Tbsp olive oil
juice of ½ lemon, or more if needed
sea salt and freshly ground black pepper

Place all the ingredients into your most powerful blender.

Process into a smooth dip or pâté, adding 2 to 3 Tbsp of water and a little more lemon juice if necessary to help it along. Serve with any crudités you want.

Almond cookies

These simple cookies prove that sometimes you really can have your cake and eat it. Simple and straightforward, while the smell that fills the kitchen when these are cooking ... oh my.

MAKES 8 TO 10

7 Tbsp (100 g) unsalted butter
2½ cups (250 g) ground almonds
1 tsp stevia
1 tsp vanilla extract
1 egg, lightly beaten, plus more to brush
handful of skin-on almonds, chopped

Preheat the oven to 300°F/150°C.

Cream the butter with a fork in a bowl. Add the remaining ingredients (except the chopped almonds) and mix well to form a dough.

Roll into eight to 10 small balls. Place on a baking sheet, then press each down to form a cookie, leaving a small amount of space between each. Brush with egg and sprinkle with the chopped almonds.

Bake in the oven for around 20 minutes, or until starting to turn golden brown.

Transfer to a wire rack with a palette knife and let cool completely.

Peanut butter protein bars These bars are a great gooey, feel-good snack that ticks the sweet boxes, yet keeps blood sugar nice and even. As always, choose a low-carb whey protein that doesn't have the silly amounts of added sugar. Also use a good-quality pure peanut butter, not one with buckets of added sugar and salt.

MAKES 8 TO 10
2 heaping Tbsp coconut oil
1½ cups (340 g) peanut butter
2 scoops vanilla whey protein
2 tsp mixed seeds

Melt the coconut oil gently in a small pan.

Mix the peanut butter, whey protein, and seeds together well. Pour over the coconut oil, then stir well again.

This should give you a stickyish dough that is pliable and easy to work with. Place this dough into a container such as an old ice-cream tub. Push the dough firmly down. Place the container in the refrigerator and refrigerate overnight, before cutting into bars. Make sure you don't cut the bars too big and eat just one a day.

Spiced chocolate cashews

These are an awesome little snack. Great as an opener at a dinner party, or perfect refrigerator door snacks for when the chocolate craving hits. Keep it to five or six as a snack between meals.

MAKES ABOUT 8 SERVINGS

3½ oz (100 g) 80 percent cocoa solids semisweet chocolate
⅔ cup cup (80 g) raw cashews
pinch of ground cinnamon
pinch of chili powder

Half fill a saucepan with boiled water.

Place a heatproof glass bowl over the water, making sure it doesn't touch the water, and break the chocolate into the bowl. Stir continuously until the chocolate melts.

Add the cashews, cinnamon, and chili powder and mix well so the chocolate coats all of the nuts.

Lay out a sheet of wax paper and place the coated nuts onto it. Let cool fully.

INDEX

Thai green vegetable 118
dal, garden pea 126
DHA 54
digestion 19–25
disaccharides 20, 22
dressing, citrus omega 90

eggs: avocado, cilantro, and
    cheddar omelet 74
  egg & watercress rye open sandwich 84
  kipper kedgeree 72
  low-carb eggs royale 76
  mixed greens and poached egg stack 70
  salad Niçoise with chicken 81
  smoked salmon, spinach, dill omelet 71
  Spanish scramble 67
  spinach baked eggs 92
EPA 54

fat, body 29, 34–5
fats 17, 24–5, 50–1
fatty acids 35–7, 51–8
fava bean, mint, and feta salad 82
fennel: peppered cod with barlotto 110
  sea bass with roasted fennel and
    spiced root vegetable mash 120
  white beans with spinach, roasted
    fennel and garlic 104
fiber 20
fish 56, 57–8, 59
  see also cod; salmon, etc
food combining 19, 49–51
frittata, mixed vegetable 66
fructose 22
fruit 49

garlic: seafood fried rice with
    garlic greens 122
  white beans with spinach, roasted
    fennel, and garlic 104
glucagon 27
glucose 17, 20, 22–3, 26–30, 32–9
glucotoxicity 36–7
glycemic index 41–4
glycated hemoglobin 39
glycogen 23, 26, 27, 29

goji berries, stir-fried shrimp, and
    zucchini ribbons with cashews and 89
greens: king shrimp and greens in
    satay sauce 100
  omega herb-crusted salmon, spiced
    sweet potato mash, wilted greens 114
  pesto-roast salmon, buttered greens 101
  seafood fried rice with garlic greens 122

halloumi: griddled halloumi with roasted
    vegetables and seeded quinoa 94
HBA1C 39
high blood pressure 36
high blood sugar 27, 29
houmous: minted beet houmous
    and goat cheese salad bowl 88
hyperglycemia 34, 36

inflammation 53–4, 58
insulin 8, 17, 29, 30, 44
  insulin resistance 31–7, 40–4
  and omega 3 54–5
insulin receptors 29, 32, 34, 43, 44, 54, 58
intestines 22–5
inulin 58

kedgeree, kipper 72
Keys, Ancel 44–5, 51

lactase 22
lactose 22
Langerhans 30, 36
large intestine 23
LDL cholesterol 36
leeks: cod, leek puree and green salad 128
lemongrass chicken stew 112
lentils: bacon-wrapped chicken breast
    with herbed spinach Puy lentils 124
  lentil and bacon soup 78
  speedy chicken and lentil curry 96
lifestyle and diabetes 10
ligand 15
limes: citrus omega dressing 90
lipases 24, 25
lipogenesis 29, 35
lipoproteins 35

Clare Hulton—we are really cooking on gas now! Amazing work. Thank you! Jenny Liddle—you are tireless at what you do! Tanya Murkett—as always, supporting me and putting up with me no matter what! A big thank you to all the team at Quadrille, Smith & Gilmour, Martin Poole, and Aya Nishimura. Catherine Tyldesley, Gaby Roslin, and all of the wonderful people that have supported my work and career. Ramsay and Candy. Mom and Dad.

Editorial director: Anne Furniss
Creative director: Helen Lewis
Project editor: Lucy Bannell
Art direction and design: Smith & Gilmour
Photography: Martin Poole
Illustration: Blindsalida
Food stylist: Aya Nishimura
Props stylists: Polly Webb-Wilson & Wei Tang
Production: Tom Moore

This edition first published in 2018 by Quadrille,
an imprint of Hardie Grant Publishing

Quadrille
Pentagon House,
52–54 Southwark Street
London SE1 1UN
quadrille.com

Cataloguing in Publication Data: a catalogue record for this book is available from the British Library.

978 1 78713 142 2

Printed in China